W9-AUJ-471

Social Issues
in Literature

Sexuality in
the Comedies of
William Shakespeare

Other Books in the Social Issues in Literature Series:

OPPOSING
VIEWPOINTS®
SERIES

Sexuality in the Comedies of William Shakespeare

Stephen P. Thompson, Book Editor

GREENHAVEN PRESS
A part of Gale, Cengage Learning

GALE
CENGAGE Learning·

Farmington Hills, Mich • San Francisco • New York • Waterville, Maine
Meriden, Conn • Mason, Ohio • Chicago

Elizabeth Des Chenes, *Director, Content Strategy*
Cynthia Sanner, *Publisher*
Douglas Dentino, *Manager, New Product*

Articles in Greenhaven Press anthologies are often edited for length to meet page requirements. In addition, original titles of these works are changed to clearly present the main thesis and to explicitly indicate the author's opinion. Every effort is made to ensure that Greenhaven Press accurately reflects the original intent of the authors. Every effort has been made to trace the owners of copyrighted material.

Cover image © Classic Image/Alamy.

LIBRARY OF CONGRESS CATALOGING-IN-PUBLICATION DATA

Sexuality in the comedies of William Shakespeare / Stephen P. Thompson, book editor.
    pages cm. -- (Social issues in literature)
    Summary: "Social Issues in Literature meets the need for materials supporting curriculum integration. Each title in this distinctive new series examines an important literary work or body of work through the lens of a major social issue. Each volume presents biographical and critical information on the author, viewpoints on the social issue portrayed in the book, and contemporary assessments of the social issue as well as a chronology of important dates in the author's life, discussion questions, a guide to additional literary works that focus on the same social issue, a bibliography for further research and a thorough subject index"-- Provided by publisher.
    Includes bibliographical references and index.
    ISBN 978-0-7377-6982-1 (hardback)
    ISBN 978-0-7377-6983-8 (paperback)
    1. Shakespeare, William, 1564-1616--Comedies--Juvenile literature. 2. Sex in literature--Juvenile literature. 3. Love in literature--Juvenile literature. 4. Marriage in literature--Juvenile literature. 5. Sex role in literature--Juvenile literature. 6. Sex differences (Psychology)--Juvenile literature. 7. Sexual orientation in literature--Juvenile literature. 8. Courtship in literature--Juvenile literature. I. Thompson, Stephen P., 1953- editor of compilation.
    PR2981.S395 2014
    822.3'3--dc23
                                                                    2013036320

Contents

Courtship in Shakespeare's comedies is an ambiguous, sometimes chaotic, phase of life for young people. Their expressions of desire and sexuality are ultimately brought under control through the institution of marriage, which exists to regulate sexual conduct.

When Rosalind in *As You Like It* takes on the disguise of
a shepherd boy, she is freed from conventional constraints
on female behavior in courtship, and she takes the lead
in wooing Orlando and in educating him about the con-
nection between desire and love.

Chapter 3: Sexuality in the Twenty-First Century

Introduction

A young man who is engaged to be married gets his fiancée pregnant. A zealous, fundamentalist judge decides to prosecute the couple for sexual immorality based on an obscure law still on the books. When the young man's beautiful sister comes to plead her brother's case, the zealous judge propositions her, offering to free her brother in exchange for sex. Meanwhile, recently arrested pimps and prostitutes argue that their occupation actually benefits society. Is this the plot of a recent soap opera on television, or a recent far-fetched romantic comedy? Actually, it is neither. This is the plot of William Shakespeare's *Measure for Measure*, written at the peak of his creativity, right after *Hamlet*, and right before *King Lear* and *Macbeth*. Throughout his career, in his sonnets as well as in his plays, Shakespeare explored sexuality and issues of sexual behavior.

In the present, the term "sexuality" is taken to encompass the full range of sexual behavior and interaction that occurs in Shakespeare's comedies. Sexuality in these plays is expressed through courtship rituals, sexual wordplay and innuendo, sappy love poetry, gender-role confusion, cross-dressing, attempted rape, bed-substitution tricks, premarital pregnancy, prostitution, spontaneous marriages, and enforced marriages. The end point of virtually all the sexual behavior in the comedies is marriage, a social institution that had then a more secure and permanent status than it does today. However, wedding ceremonies themselves were never depicted on Shakespeare's stage, nor was the overt physicality we associate with sexual behavior. What was of interest to Shakespeare and his audiences was the journey to legitimized sexual fulfillment, a journey that explores unrequited and requited love, compatibility issues, strategies of courtship, and the issue of personal choice in marriage.

It is widely acknowledged by Shakespeare scholars that Shakespeare himself had both an unorthodox entrée into marriage as well as an unorthodox ongoing married life. It is fairly certain that eighteen-year-old William Shakespeare of Stratford-upon-Avon impregnated twenty-six-year-old Anne Hathaway prior to their marriage in November of 1582. Recent studies reveal that marriages involving bridal pregnancy were not actually uncommon in Shakespeare's day, but the records also confirm that it was rare for a child to be born out of wedlock. Though there are no surviving accounts to help us characterize Shakespeare and Anne's early married life, we do know that they had three children together, one of whom, Hamnet, died at age eleven. Their two daughters, Judith and Susanna, lived to adulthood, married, and settled in Stratford. It is clear also that the marriage arrangement between Shakespeare and Anne involved long periods of separation. While Shakespeare pursued the life of the theater in London for more than twenty years, Anne remained in Stratford. Shakespeare did, however, retire to Stratford for the last five years or so of his life, and there he died.

Shakespeare and his audiences clearly found relationships between the sexes to be fascinating, and Shakespeare entertained his audiences with many variations of the classic "boy meets girl" plot. Not all characters get the proverbial happy ending, though. As scholar David Bevington observes in *Shakespeare and Biography*, "Love in these romantic comedies is ecstatic, but it is also a battlefield strewn with wounded participants." Two early plays that are often paired, *Romeo and Juliet* and *A Midsummer Night's Dream*, depict the sexual passions of young love and desire, one play with a tragic ending, and one with a happy ending. Containing literature's most famous depiction of "love at first sight," *Romeo and Juliet* depicts two young lovers so intensely passionate that it is impossible to draw a line between their sexual passion and their love. In order to be able to sleep together—and because their families would disapprove of their match—they are married secretly. The lengths they take to escape parental disapproval lead to tragedy. In *A Midsummer Night's Dream*, four young lovers, seeking to evade parental control of their marriage decisions, escape into the woods at night, where the "madness" of young lust and the delusions of infatuation are somehow magically resolved into the harmony of marriage.

One of the innovations that marked Shakespeare as ahead of his time is his elevated portrayal of women and their sexuality, especially the heroines of his romantic comedies. He consistently makes his female lead characters intelligent, witty, resourceful, and sensible, easily a match for the men they fall in love with. In *As You Like It*, for example, Rosalind is able to make sexual puns as well as any man, but she is also insightful enough to see through the insincerity and shallowness of conventional courtship rhetoric and poetry. In *Much Ado About Nothing*, the heroine Beatrice is able to hold her own in a sarcastic "wit combat" with her male counterpart, Benedick. Both Beatrice and Benedick fear that marriage will rob them of their freedom and individuality; therefore, they must be tricked by their friends, who can see what a perfect match in temperament they really are. Though it would be a stretch to call his depiction of women a call for "equality" in the modern sense, Shakespeare certainly depicts mutuality, compatibility, and harmony between the sexes as a goal in sexual relations and marriage. These and other issues of sexuality in Shakespeare's comedies are explored in the essays that follow. Chapter one focuses on Shakespeare's life, chapter two on sexuality in Shakespeare's comedies, and chapter three on sexuality in the twenty-first century.

Chronology

1564

William Shakespeare is baptized in Stratford-upon-Avon on April 26 and is presumed to have been born three days prior, on April 23. Christopher Marlowe is born in Canterbury, on February 26.

1569

Shakespeare's father, John, a leather goods craftsman, serves one term as bailiff (equivalent of mayor) of Stratford after having served three years on the town council.

1576

The first public playhouse, the Theatre, opens in London.

1582

William Shakespeare marries Anne Hathaway.

1583

The Shakespeares' first child, Susanna, is born.

1585

The Shakespeares' twins, Judith and Hamnet, named after neighbors and friends Judith and Hamnet Sadler, are born.

1588

The Spanish Armada is defeated, and the attempted invasion of England is thwarted.

c. 1589

Shakespeare's rival, playwright Christopher Marlowe, writes *Doctor Faustus*, the most popular play of the years contemporaneous with Shakespeare's early hits.

c. 1589–1591

Shakespeare's first two hit plays—*Henry VI, Part 1* and *Titus Andronicus*—are performed.

1592

A pamphlet that includes an attack on Shakespeare as an "upstart crow" is first evidence that Shakespeare has been writing plays in London. The Rose Theatre opens on the South Bank.

1592–1594

All public playhouses in London are closed for nearly two years due to an outbreak of the plague.

1593

Shakespeare's long narrative poem *Venus and Adonis*, his most popular printed work during his lifetime, is published. Christopher Marlowe is killed in a tavern brawl. The play *The Taming of the Shrew* is first performed.

1594

Along with seven fellow actors and investors, Shakespeare forms the Lord Chamberlain's Men as a profit-sharing acting company. Lord Chamberlain's Men first perform for Queen Elizabeth.

c. 1594–1595

The plays *A Midsummer Night's Dream*, *Love's Labour's Lost*, and *Romeo and Juliet* are first performed.

1596

Through William Shakespeare's success, a coat of arms is granted to Shakespeare's father, John, raising his rank in society to "gentleman." Shakespeare's son, Hamnet, dies at age eleven.

1597

Shakespeare's purchase of the large house New Place in Stratford demonstrates his early financial success.

c. 1597–1598

The plays *Henry IV, Part 1* and *Much Ado About Nothing* are first performed.

1599

The Lord Chamberlain's Men dismantle the Theatre and move it south across the Thames River. They re-erect it on the South Bank and rename it the Globe Theatre. The plays *As You Like It*, *Henry V*, and *Julius Caesar* are written.

c. 1600–1601

The plays *Hamlet* and *The Merry Wives of Windsor* are first performed.

1602

Shakespeare makes a large purchase of land in Stratford.

1603

Queen Elizabeth dies. Shakespeare and his company of actors receive the patronage of the new sovereign, King James I, and are renamed the King's Men. The King's Men march in the new king's coronation procession in early 1604.

1604

The plays *Measure for Measure* and *Othello* are first performed.

c. 1605–1606

The plays *King Lear* and *Macbeth* are first performed.

1607

Daughter Susanna marries the Stratford town physician, Dr. John Hall.

1608

The King's Men begin performing in the indoor Blackfriars Theatre, which they own.

1609

Shakespeare's *Sonnets* is published.

1611

The King James version of the Bible is published. The play *The Tempest* is produced.

c. 1612–1613

Shakespeare retires to Stratford-upon-Avon, but also buys a house near the Blackfriars Theatre in London.

1613

The Globe Theatre burns to the ground after catching fire during a performance of *Henry VIII*. It is rebuilt by June 1614.

1616

Daughter Judith marries Thomas Quiney. Shakespeare dies in Stratford, at the age of 52.

1623

Thirty-six of Shakespeare's plays are collected and published in the *First Folio*. Anne Hathaway Shakespeare dies in Stratford, at age 67.

Background on
William Shakespeare

The Life of Shakespeare

David Scott Kastan

David Scott Kastan, professor of English at Columbia University, is the author of Shakespeare and the Book *(2001) and several other books on Shakespeare. He has edited many of Shakespeare's plays, and he is also editor of* A Companion to Shakespeare *(1999).*

In the following viewpoint, Kastan reviews the known facts and main events of Shakespeare's life, beginning with his baptism in 1564, his marriage to Anne Hathaway in 1582, and the births of his three children. Kastan discusses Shakespeare's middle-class parents, John and Mary, and his education in Stratford. Above all, Kastan traces Shakespeare's success in the theater in London as a writer of popular plays. Though Shakespeare found fame as a playwright, his considerable financial success came only through his investment as a shareholder in his acting company, the Lord Chamberlain's Men.

William Shakespeare is the best-known author in the English-speaking world. His work has also been translated into more than one hundred languages, and in virtually every country on earth copies of his plays can be found. Movies continue to bring his work to a new generation of admirers. Indeed, Shakespeare could be said to have started a fresh career as a successful film writer; between 1989 and 1999 alone, nine major motion pictures were made from his plays. This is testimony to the enduring appeal of his characters and plots. His Hollywood success may perhaps come as a surprise to many who revere him as the greatest of our literary figures, but it is a success that would no doubt have delighted him.

David Scott Kastan, "William Shakespeare," *World Poets*, ed. Ron Padgett. New York: Charles Scribner's Sons, 2000, pp. 477–486. From, *World Poets*. © Cengage Learning. Reproduced by permission.

In truth, Shakespeare had small literary ambition for his plays. He was primarily a man of the theater: an actor, a playwright, and a "sharer" (a part owner) in the acting company for which he wrote—the Lord Chamberlain's Men, which became the King's Men soon after James I became king of England in 1603. The profits of the acting company brought him substantial rewards, but he did not receive royalties or commissions on what he wrote. The only form of public recognition he actively sought for his plays was their performance. Although nineteen were published in his lifetime, not one was published with his involvement, and, indeed, the first few were printed with no indication of his authorship.

This is not, however, as surprising as it perhaps seems to us. Plays then were subliterary, the products of an emerging entertainment industry that was dominated by star actors. Revealingly, the two narrative poems that Shakespeare wrote, *Venus and Adonis* and *The Rape of Lucrece*, appeared in carefully printed editions to which Shakespeare contributed elaborate dedications. Meanwhile, the plays were published in cheap, poorly printed editions with no regard for the quality of the texts. The plays reached their publishers in various ways; usually they were purchased from the acting company for which they were written and to which they belonged. In the absence of anything like our modern copyright laws, this practice was all perfectly legal. Shakespeare seems to have been unconcerned about these early editions. Only after his death (1616) was there an effort to publish a substantial volume of his work. Two friends and fellow actors, John Heminges and Henry Condell, joined with a group of publishers to produce a large, expensive collected edition (1623), known today as the *First Folio*. This book contains thirty-six of Shakespeare's plays, eighteen of which had not previously appeared in print. Heminges and Condell offered the book to the buying public, as they said in its dedication, not for their "self-profit" or "fame" but "only to keep the memory of so worthy a Friend and Fellow alive."

The Authorship Controversy

With the publication of the *First Folio*, Shakespeare truly entered English history as a literary figure—his reputation and artistic achievement were secure. Nonetheless there are some who, awed by the accomplishment, passionately believe that someone other than Shakespeare was the author of the works attributed to him. In truth, little recommends this belief, except unintended humor. Some anti-Stratfordians (as those who deny Shakespeare's authorship are often called, with a reference to Shakespeare's birthplace) have had unfortunate names like Looney, Battey, and Silliman.

The argument that someone other than Shakespeare wrote the plays is based less on evidence than on social snobbery—a conviction that only a person educated at court or at a university would be capable of such remarkable artistry. But Shakespeare's life is not, in its broad outlines, much different from the lives of the other major writers of the Renaissance. Like Shakespeare, most came from the lower middle class and were not university educated (and it should be recalled that a university education then was highly specialized, preparing students mainly for the church or government service).

The Facts of Shakespeare's Life

We know a remarkable amount about Shakespeare, considering how long ago he lived. He was born in late April of 1564 in Stratford-upon-Avon, a small market town in England. The parish church there records his baptism on 26 April, and his unrecorded birthday has been plausibly set three days earlier, on 23 April, Saint George's Day (which also, apparently, was the date of his death fifty-two years later). His father was John Shakespeare, a glover and later a wool merchant; his mother was Mary Arden, daughter of a successful farmer in the nearby village of Wilmcote. Although the records have not survived, we can safely assume he attended the King's New School, the Stratford grammar school, with its strenuous, classically based curriculum. We know for certain that at age eighteen he married Anne Hathaway of Stratford and that a daughter, Susanna, was born to them on 26 May 1583. On 2 February 1585 Anne gave birth to twins: Hamnet and Judith.

Sometime after the birth of the twins, Shakespeare left Stratford for London, where, by the early 1590s, he was well established in the theater. References to his theatrical activity abound, and in 1598, Francis Meres in his *Palladis Tamia: Wit's Treasury* (London, 1598, f. 281) claimed that Shakespeare could be compared to the ancient Roman playwrights Seneca for tragedy and Plautus for comedy and that among English writers he was the best of "both kinds for the stage." Friends commented on his modesty and good nature; tax records reveal his financial success. In 1597 he bought a substantial house in Stratford for sixty pounds (the equivalent of about thirty thousand dollars today). In 1602 he purchased 107 acres north of the town for £320. In 1605 he bought a half-interest in a Stratford farm for £440, and in 1613, with three other investors, he acquired a house in Blackfriars, a district in London, for £140. These considerable sums testify to the prosperity that came with his life in the theater.

Shakespeare died in late April of 1616 and was buried on the north side of the chancel of Holy Trinity. His will has survived, in which he left £10 for "the poor of Stratford," remembered friends, and provided for his family. He left money to buy memorial rings for three surviving members of his acting company: Richard Burbage, John Heminges, and Henry Condell (the last two were the "editors" of the *First Folio*). He left £150 to his daughter Judith, and another £150 to be paid if "she or any issue of her body be living" three years after the execution of the will. The bulk of the estate was left to Susanna. Shakespeare's wife is mentioned only once, in an apparent afterthought to the document: "Item, I give unto my wife my second best bed with the furniture." The strange bequest has led some to speculate that this was a deliberate slight, but

English customary law provided the widow with one-third of the estate, and the "second best bed" was almost certainly their own, the best being reserved for guests.

Shakespeare's Poetry

Still, whatever we know about Shakespeare's life can hardly explain the accomplishment of his writing. The two narrative poems; the poem *The Phoenix and the Turtle*; the edition of 154 sonnets, along with "A Lover's Complaint" (first published in 1609); and the thirty-eight plays form an unrivaled body of work. While today the poetry, except for the sonnets, is not much read, in Shakespeare's time the poems were much admired. Francis Meres, in 1598 (*Palladis Tamia*, f. 281), called him "mellifluous and honey-tongued Shakespeare," especially noting "his *Venus and Adonis*, his *Lucrece*, his sugared Sonnets among his private friends" (referring to the fact that they were not yet in print but circulating in manuscripts).

The sonnets, however, have become the best known of his nondramatic verse. Two were published in 1599 in a collection of contemporary poetry called *The Passionate Pilgrim*, but it was not until 1609 that all the sonnets were in print. That year Thomas Thorpe published a book titled *Shakespeare's Sonnets*, which included 154 sonnets and a longer poem, "A Lover's Complaint." The sonnets have been mined for evidence about Shakespeare's life, as scholars have debated who was the dark lady (see sonnet 127) and who was Shakespeare's "fair friend" (sonnet 104), but in truth the sonnets' value lies in their more general insight into human emotion. They are wonderful poems that give voice to both the bitter and the sweet experiences of human love.

The Plays

Shakespeare's plays prove how much he is indeed, as his friend the dramatist Ben Jonson said in a poem in the 1623 folio of Shakespeare's plays, "not of an age, but for all time." His dra-

A nineteenth-century illustration of Shakespeare reciting one of his plays to his family in Stratford-upon-Avon. A scene such as this rarely occurred, as Shakespeare spent most of his married life in London, while his family remained in Stratford. © Michael Nicholson/ Corbis.

matic career was long and uniquely successful. He wrote comedies, tragedies, and history plays; in each genre he began by mastering the conventions he inherited and gradually pushed the form to achieve more than it had ever been asked to do.

The Comedies

With comedy, for example, he began by writing a conventional (and very funny) play, *The Comedy of Errors*. Based on a model of classical Roman comedy, the play is a riotous farce about the mistaken identities of two sets of twins. But the complication that produces the comedy is completely external: once the twins are correctly sorted out, all social relations happily reassume their customary shape. The middle comedies—*A Midsummer Night's Dream, Much Ado About Nothing,* and *Twelfth Night*—all use the comic form brilliantly to explore the possibilities of romantic love, as young lovers learn to trust the heart's logic over the less generous social logic of the communities in which they live.

In the later comedies, however, the romantic conclusions grew more tentative and fragile, more obviously artificial and forced. There is little of the sense of celebration that marks the resolution of the earlier comedies. "All is well ended," says the king in the epilogue to *All's Well That Ends Well*, "if this suit be won: / That you express content." Yet content is not exactly what we feel at the play's end; rather we feel that the comic conclusion is awkward and compromised, more like life than comedy.

The History Plays

Similarly, in writing history plays Shakespeare stretches the form to perform new and more ambitious tasks. Where the few pre-Shakespearean history plays were for the most part patriotic celebrations, some written in response to the extraordinary victory of the English fleet over the Spanish Armada in 1588, Shakespeare's ten plays on English historical subjects use the form to examine the nature of authority and of Englishness itself. The four early plays—the three parts of *Henry VI* as well as *Richard III*—treat the end of the royal house of Plantagenet that had ruled in England from 1154 to 1399. The unseemly struggles for the throne among rival aristocratic houses mock the pious rhetoric and graceful ceremonies of rule. When Richard III takes the throne through a series of outrageously wicked acts, he functions not only as a villain but as a scourge to purge the land of those who have sullied it with their ambition. In turn, he is destroyed by Henry, earl of Richmond, who is crowned Henry VII. The first of the Tudor monarchs, Henry plays the role of England's savior in a divine drama of retribution and renewal.

The later histories—another sequence of four plays, *Richard II*, the two parts of *Henry IV*, and *Henry V*—are less confident about God's role in English history. They depict a thoroughly secular world of human drive and desire unredeemed by divine sanction or perspective. Even Henry V, the most successful of Shakespeare's kings, reveals the heavy moral price that political success exacts. Shakespeare knows well that the fallible humanity of even this "mirror of all Christian kings" (act II, chorus, line 6) makes large the gap between the ideal and the real.

The Tragedies

The tragedies remain Shakespeare's most powerful exploration of what it means to be human. Again, he began with conventional models: the violent action of *Titus Andronicus* brilliantly animates the inherited revenge patterns of Senecan drama and its Elizabethan imitators, and the lyrical *Romeo and Juliet* finds tragedy in the poignancy of thwarted love. Gradually, however, Shakespeare moved past his literary models and wrote powerful plays uniquely his own, even when they took the stories of earlier writers for sources. *Hamlet, King Lear, Othello*, and *Macbeth*, the four tragedies upon which Shakespeare's reputation most fully rests, are the most powerful of these. Every age has felt obligated to confront and claim these plays for itself. "Who is it that can tell me who I am?" asks King Lear; for many, the answer is Shakespeare in these four plays. Shakespeare's last tragedies, *Timon of Athens* and *Coriolanus*, both written around 1607, take the tragic logic one step further, denying the audience even the solace of the poetic richness that marks the four major tragedies. Timon and Coriolanus are destroyed by their rigidity, and their fall is unredeemed by either self-knowledge or the consolations of art.

The Final Four

The four last plays, *Pericles, [Prince of Tyre], Cymbeline, The Winter's Tale*, and *The Tempest*, all written between 1608 and 1611, attempt something different. *The Winter's Tale* and *The Tempest* are grouped among the comedies in the *First Folio*, *Cymbeline* is placed among the tragedies, and *Pericles* does not appear at all until a reissue of a third edition in 1663. This history alone points to their experimental qualities. Later critics have termed them "romances" or "tragicomedies," plays that let the audience experience the losses in the tragedies but that also offer a vision of forgiveness. In tragedy, time destroys, and death is the central and unavoidable fact. In the romances, though there is loss, there is also consolation and the promise of renewal. Before he dies, King Lear directs attention to the lifeless body of his daughter Cordelia: "Do you see this? Look on her! Look, her lips. / Look there, look there." Near the end of *The Winter's Tale*, our attention is directed to another woman, as Paulina unveils what seems to be a statue of the supposedly dead Hermione and asks all assembled to "Behold, and say 'tis well." Cordelia is "gone forever," but Hermione lives again. In the romances loss gives way to gain. "Go together," Paulina urges, "You precious winners all." Not only the romances but all of Shakespeare's works make those who fully experience them just such "precious winners."

The Ambiguous Sexuality of Shakespeare's Sonnets

Robert Matz

Robert Matz is professor of English and chair of the English Department at George Mason University. Author of numerous books and essays on English Renaissance literature, his most recent book is The World of Shakespeare's Sonnets: An Introduction *(2008).*

As Robert Matz points out in the following viewpoint, Shakespeare scholars are largely in agreement that a significant portion of Shakespeare's sonnets are addressed to a man. Since many of these same sonnets contain expressions of devotion, even love, many current scholars conclude that Shakespeare must have been gay, or at least bisexual. Other scholars, including Matz, contend that reading the sonnets as autobiographical can be limiting and misleading since same-sex affection was not necessarily viewed then as it is now. Matz notes many of the cultural differences between modern-day ideas of same-sex love and Renaissance ideas on the subject.

"Not marble nor the gilded monuments / Of princes shall outlive this powerful rhyme." Shakespeare's famous promise in sonnet 55 to preserve the memory of his beloved echoes in sonnet 63: "His beauty shall in these black lines be seen / And they shall live, and he in them still green." But sonnet 63 makes clear the beloved's sex: "His beauty." Many people remain unaware that the first 126 of Shakespeare's 154 sonnets pay tribute to his love for a man. Contemporary representations of the sonnets often encourage this misapprehension.

The difference between poetry and perception is especially great because readers usually prize the sonnets written for the man rather than for the woman. The group of sonnets written for the man celebrates a romantic love that resists change in time, fortune, or heart. This is Shakespeare as we like him: "Shall I compare thee to a summer's day" (sonnet 18), "You live in this, and dwell in lovers' eyes" (sonnet 55); "Let me not to the marriage of true minds / Admit impediments" (sonnet 116). The sonnets written about a woman are different and less quotable—if one's aim is endearment. Love in these sonnets is cynical, even disgusted. Has any lover ever sent a carefully handwritten copy of sonnet 129 ("Th'expense of spirit in a waste of shame / Is lust in action") along with a dozen roses? Has any wedding service ever included a reading of sonnet 138: "When my love swears that she is made of truth / I do believe her though I know she lies"?

On learning that many of the sonnets commemorate Shakespeare's love for a man people frequently wonder whether Shakespeare was gay. And largely because of the sonnets Shakespeare's name sometimes appears in lists of famous gay authors or historical figures. There is something to be said for these autobiographical readings. Imagining the sonnets as the place where Shakespeare reveals his gay identity (as well as his adulterous, cross-class and, as we shall see, possibly cross-racial loves) provides a tonic to bland characterizations of Shakespeare as an icon of cultural conservatism.

Still, reading the sonnets as autobiography has its problems. We cannot with certainty identify the young man or black mistress, or the degree of physical intimacy Shakespeare had with either. The sonnets to the black mistress sound more sexual than the sonnets to the young man. But the language of love to the young man hardly rules out sex, just as the sexual language about the black mistress cannot prove that Shakespeare really had sex with her.

Cultural Differences About Sexuality

More importantly, autobiographical readings of the sonnets are limiting. The focus on Shakespeare the man may short-circuit the difference of culture and treat Shakespeare as if he were our contemporary. We need rather a sense of the cultural differences between ideas of sexuality in Shakespeare's time and in our own. Identifying Shakespeare as gay from an auto-biographical reading of the sonnets is particularly misleading, since the term evokes a contemporary idea of fixed sexual identity that the Renaissance did not share. The term "gay" (or "homosexual") has other limitations as well. It reduces the same-sex love in the sonnets to a modern, personal category rather than recognizing its importance to the world of patronage and social status recounted in the previous section of this [viewpoint]. And it implies that same-sex love was viewed in the English Renaissance, as it often is today, as subversive or transgressive of orthodox morality. As we will see, it was just the opposite.

Rather than treating the sonnets in narrowly biographical terms I frame my discussion of Shakespeare's relationship to the young man around the different understandings of love between men in the Renaissance and today. Nor do I focus only on whether the sonnets reveal a sexual relationship with the young man—a topic frequently debated in discussions of these sonnets—though in the final chapter of this section I do consider the matter. The question of whether two people had sex is usually interesting, but so too is the historically different experience of love and desire expressed in Shakespeare's relationship to the young man.

As the fight over gay marriage in the U.S. and elsewhere intensifies, the stakes in this history are high. Objecting to gay marriage, social and religious conservatives invoke a traditional conception of marriage as between one man and one woman. These traditionalists, as Katha Pollitt observes, ignore the wide variety of marriage traditions in the past five thousand years of Western history. Enter Shakespeare's sonnets, which neglect all the way to adultery Shakespeare's legal and child-bearing marriage to Anne Hathaway, while celebrating a marriage between men based on the love they share. These aspects of the sonnet story become more important if they are seen not as biography, as clues to Shakespeare's particular emotional and sexual life, but as evidence of the changing historical understandings of love and marriage. "Let me not to the marriage of true minds / Admit impediments" may not be Shakespeare's bumper-sticker take on the debate over gay marriage. But the history reflected in the sonnets should be part of that debate.

The Term "Homosexual"

The sonnets, which never define themselves as "homosexual" poetry, suggest the variability of our conceptions of same-sex desire. To start with, there were no "homosexuals" in Renaissance England—and no "heterosexuals" either. Both these terms date from the late nineteenth century. Why didn't these words (or similar ones) exist earlier, since they now seem so indispensable for categorizing people and dividing up sexual desire? Historians have argued that not just the words "homosexual" and "heterosexual" are missing, but the kinds of people they describe.

Of course, people of the same sex had sexual relations before the invention of the term "homosexual." But they understood and experienced those relations differently. The word often used to describe sex between men was "sodomy," which meant something substantially different than the latter category of the homosexual. . . .

Sex and Sinfulness

Sodomy in the Renaissance was considered morally wrong and it was illegal. Conviction of sodomy was punishable by death. But evidence from court records indicates that homo-

William Shakespeare, English poet and playwright. © GL Archive/Alamy.

sexual sex was rarely punished or even prosecuted during the period. Moralists and laws said one thing. What people did and what happened to them was another.

This contradiction reflects the fact that in any society the meanings and morality attributed to sexual acts vary widely, and English Renaissance society was no exception to this rule. On the one hand, since in the Renaissance all sex outside marriage was sinful—even sex within marriage was not clearly free of sin—homosexual sex could be viewed as one sexual transgression among many. It was wrong, but so was fornication—heterosexual sex outside of marriage. Practically speaking, fornication in fact presented more of a problem than homosexual sex. Authorities were more worried about sex that would result in illegitimate children, for which the community would have to provide.

On the other hand, sodomy could be singled out for special condemnation. It was declared monstrous, a treason against God and country, akin to witchcraft and sorcery. Often in such cases it was associated with persons felt to threaten established order, such as Catholics or foreigners. Yet these condemnations may also have created a break between this official morality and ordinary sexual practice. Did such terrible offenses, committed by dangerous men, have anything to do with a little messing around among friends? According to a 1991 study, about 60% of contemporary U.S. college students did not define engaging in oral sex as having "had sex"; for various kinds of foreplay the percentage is much lower still. Likewise, "ordinary" (or privileged) men in Renaissance England could engage in sexual activity with one another and not see themselves, or find themselves prosecuted as, monstrous sodomites. Even English Renaissance legal authorities did not view most same-sex sexual relations as prosecutable sodomy. . . .

Love Between Men

Men having sex with one another in Shakespeare's day would not have tried to puzzle out whether they were gay. Nor would they usually have feared prosecution. To these contexts for Shakespeare's sonnets to the young man we can add the most important of all: Renaissance English culture placed a high value on the love between men.

Male same-sex love in the English Renaissance was not marginal or subversive. It was integral to some of the most cherished aspects of English cultural life, and to England's most important political institutions. Just as the sin of sodomy was not seen as the expression of a distinct sexual identity, neither was the celebrated virtue of male love. This love, rather, was part of a man's place in particular cultural and social worlds, where it affirmed his public, social or political bonds with another man.

Social Issues in Literature

CHAPTER 2

Sexuality in Shakespeare's Comedies

Shakespeare's Ideas on Sex and Gender

David Bevington

A prominent American scholar of Shakespeare, David Bevington is longtime professor of the humanities at the University of Chicago. He is editor of The Complete Works of Shakespeare *(seventh edition, 2013) and has edited and written about many works of Renaissance literature. Among his recent books is* Murder Most Foul: Hamlet Through the Ages *(2011).*

In the view of David Bevington, the heroines of Shakespeare's romantic comedies are consistently more mature, socially and emotionally, than are the male characters. With their better self-knowledge and sharper wit, they must lead the male characters to a more complete understanding of their sexuality and of love before they will submit to marriage. These heroines frequently use a disguise as a man to assist them in their task of male education.

Generally, in [Shakespeare's] romantic comedies of the 1590s, the young women are much better at knowing themselves than are the young men. The women are plucky, patient, and good-humoured. They seem to enjoy teasing their young men, but do so knowing that they will submit themselves finally to their wooers. Marriage will put women in a subordinate position. They are aware of this, and accept the conditions of a patriarchal culture. They are intent on marriage, and generally know right away whom it is that they will marry. Although the men nominally take the lead in proposing marriage, the women are better aware of what is at stake.

David Bevington, *Shakespeare's Ideas: More Things in Heaven and Earth*. Oxford: Wiley-Blackwell, 2008, pp. 23–31. Copyright © 2008 by Wiley Publishing. All rights reserved. Reproduced by permission.

The women seem smarter and more self-possessed. They are wittier and blessed with an ironic sense of humour that serves them well in dealing with masculine frailty. They are ultimately forgiving.

The men, conversely, seem woefully lacking in a sensible perspective on their own desires. They flee ineffectually from romantic attachments, or mistrust the women to whom they are attracted despite themselves, or are fickle in their choices. They seem far more sensitive to the judgement of their male friends then are the women to the judgement of their female peers. Their male egos are painfully insecure. A cutting remark from a woman, or a jeering laugh from a male friend, can unnerve the men utterly. Because they understand themselves so little, Shakespeare's young men can often seem absurd, even while we are invited to be sympathetic. They are their own worst enemies.

In *Love's Labour's Lost* (c.1588–97), for example, the young King of Navarre, together with Berowne and two other companions, sequester themselves in a three-year programme of study from which women are to be rigorously excluded. Romantic desire is too much of a distraction for men, they fear. Yet from the start we perceive that their resolves are hopelessly unrealistic. When the Princess of France and her entourage of three ladies appear at the entrance to Navarre on a diplomatic mission, the men have no idea what to do. Each of the four women knows instantly which of the four men is for her; never do they experience a moment's inner struggle. The men, on the other hand, go through painful contortions to hide from each other the desire they secretly are experiencing. When they are shamed into confessing to each other their weaknesses, they hit on a zany plan of disguising themselves as visiting Russians in order to pay court to the ladies, only to be mocked by the ladies for their pains and their perjuries. At the end, news of the death of the Princess gives the ladies an opportunity to postpone all romantic engagements for a year, in which time the ladies insist that the gentlemen get a better grip on themselves. The most self-aware of the young men, Berowne, freely confesses at last that he and his fellows have 'neglected time' and 'Played foul play with our oaths'. 'Your beauty, ladies, / Hath much deformed us, fashioning our humors / Even to the opposèd end of our intents', so that the gentlemen's behaviour 'hath seemed ridiculous' (5.2.751–5). The men have a lot to learn.

The four young lovers in *A Midsummer Night's Dream* (c.1595) are paired symmetrically two and two, like the four couples of *Love's Labour's Lost*, and with a similarly instructive contrast of male vs. female behaviour. The two women, Hermia and Helena, turn against each other briefly under intense pressure of sexual rivalry, but they never waver in their romantic attachments, Hermia for Lysander and Helena for Demetrius. Helena's loyalty is all the more astonishing in view of the contempt that Demetrius heaps on her for most of the play, along with a warning that he may just rape her if she doesn't stop tagging along after him in the forest. 'Use me but as your spaniel', she pleads, 'spurn me, strike me, / Neglect me, lose me; only give me leave, / Unworthy as I am, to follow you' (2.1.205–7). Hermia is similarly hurt by Lysander's desertion of her; they have eloped into the forest at great personal risk to be with each other, and now he has given her up in order that he may pursue Helena. The temporary break in friendship between Hermia and Helena is all the more painful in that they have been inseparable as childhood friends, growing together 'Like to a double cherry, seeming parted, / But yet an union in partition, / Two lovely berries molded on one stem' (3.2.209–11). The men, conversely, are constant to nothing other than to their aggressive rivalry. Demetrius, once a wooer of Helena, chases fruitlessly after Hermia, though knowing her to be in love with Lysander, until at length he is restored to his first affection. Lysander similarly shifts from his engagement with Hermia to a mad pursuit of Helena and eventually to a renewal of his first love. These changes of affection in the men are occasioned, to be sure, by the love juice that Puck squeezes on their eyes, but we are surely invited to consider the love juice as essentially a symbolic anointment betokening the proneness of the male psyche to inconstancy of affection. Lysander leaves Hermia for Helena when Hermia has demurely refused to sleep right next to Lysander on the forest floor (2.2.41–66). Demetrius remains presumably under the spell of Puck's love juice at the end of the play, suggesting that love juice acts on the male pretty much the way testosterone does. The love juice is used only on the young men, and signals their repeated shifts in choosing the female objects of their desire. . . .

Portia, in *The Merchant of Venice* (c.1596–7), is a self-possessed young woman who submits her fortunes to her father's will as specified in the competition of the three caskets, and then, having been won by Bassanio, the man she would have chosen, gracefully turns over the control of everything she has owned to her new lord and master. 'But low I was the lord / Of this fair mansion, master of my servants, / Queen o'er myself', she tells Bassanio; 'and even now, but now, / This house, these servants, and this same myself / Are yours, my lord's' (3.2.167–71). Bassanio, for his part, is a fine young man, and loyal to Portia, yet even here we encounter the comic subjection of the male. Bassanio is entirely outmanoeuvred by Portia, in her disguise as the legal expert Balthasar, into giving his wedding ring to 'Balthasar' for having saved the life of Antonio from Shylock's threat of exacting the pound of flesh. Bassanio is teased and tortured into acting out a fantasy of marital inconstancy from which Portia can release him by revealing that she herself was the learned doctor who played such a trick on him. At Belmont, in the play's comic finale, Bassanio and his male companion Gratiano are made to beg pardon of their new wives and to acknowledge that their first obligation must be to guard the sacred chastity of their marriages. Portia and Nerissa accede to the patriarchal arrangement demanded by their culture in marriage, but not without making clear their own witty superiority as a form of control. The obligations of chastely sexual union become the mirthful subject of sexual double entendre in the play's closing lines, as Gratiano vows that he will 'fear no other thing / So sore as keeping safe Nerissa's ring'; the ring is at once a symbol of chaste marriage and of the woman's sexual anatomy. No doubt 'sore' has a comically sexual resonance also. As in *Romeo and Juliet*, bawdry can be playfully entertaining in Shakespeare's romantic comedies so long as it is safely circumscribed by a happy ending in a mutually companionate marriage.

Rosalind, in *As You Like It* (1598–1600), shares many views with Portia on sex and marriage. In the play's final ceremony of multiple betrothals, Rosalind acknowledges the lordship of the two most important men in her life: her father, and Orlando, to whom she is now to be married. 'To you I give myself, for I am yours', she tells her father, and then, in the same phrasing, she says to Orlando: 'To you I give myself, for I am yours' (5.4.115–16). Her addressing them both in this fashion dramatizes the customary understanding of marriage in the Anglican Book of Common Prayer: the father gives his daughter to the younger man, transferring ownership and authority. As Prospero says in *The Tempest*, addressing Ferdinand as his prospective son-in-law: 'Then, as my gift and thine own acquisition / Worthily purchased, take my daughter' (4.1.13–14). Rosalind accepts all this, and yet she is indisputably the winner in a contest of wit between herself and Orlando. Especially at the start of the play, she is adept at badinage and wordplay whereas Orlando is ashamed at his lack of refinement and education. 'Cannot I say "I thank you"?' he wonders, when Rosalind has graciously and even invitingly given him a chain from around her own neck. . . . Rosalind must become his teacher. Her disguise in the forest as 'Ganymede' enables her to initiate a discussion on the art of wooing, in

which she hopes to instruct Orlando in how to avoid stereo-
typing and idealizing of women. He must learn that women
can be 'more clamorous than a parrot against rain, more new-
fangled than an ape'. She, posing as Orlando's Rosalind, will
be 'more giddy in my desires than a monkey. I will weep for
nothing, like Diana in the fountain, and I will do that when
you are disposed to be merry; I will laugh like a hyena, and
that when thou art inclined to sleep' (4.1.142–9). Her point is
that Orlando will be a happier and better husband if he can
begin to have a realistic understanding of what it is like for a
man and a woman to live together, day after day and year after year. Rosalind is, like so many other Shakespearean heroines, more wise, more emotionally mature, more ready for the
complexities of a real relationship than is Orlando. The same
is true in the love tragedy of *Romeo and Juliet*.

Finally, we have Viola and Orsino in *Twelfth Night*. Like
Rosalind, the resourceful Viola accepts her role as loyally obedient to her lord and master, while at the same time undertaking to educate this gentleman in all that he does not know
about courtship and marriage. Orsino is infatuated at long
distance with the Countess Olivia. Perhaps she senses, as we
do, that his ardour for her is stereotypical; Olivia is for Orsino
the unattainable goddess of a Petrarchan sonnet sequence. Being afflicted as he is with love melancholy, Orsino seems content to nurse his own exquisite suffering. His fruitless self-
abasement is not unlike that of Silvius in *As You Like It*, who
seems to ask nothing of his Phoebe other than that she allow
him to grovel in pain; the Countess Olivia is like Phoebe,
though of higher social rank, congratulating herself on the
power she enjoys through withholding of her beauty. Viola
has an answer for such sought-after beauties, which is to consider the costs to oneself of a frivolous denial of being truly in
love. 'Lady, you are the cruel'st she alive / If you will lead
these graces to the grave / And leave the world no copy', she
advises Olivia (1.5.236–8). With Orsino she proceeds much as

Actors Ian Bannen and Vanessa Redgrave portray Orlando and Rosalind, respectively, in a scene from Shakespeare's As You Like It *at London's Aldwych Theatre in 1962.* © Hulton Archive/Getty Images.

Rosalind does with Orlando, using her male guise as 'Cesario' in order that she and Orlando may talk friend to friend. 'We men may say more, swear more', she tells him, 'but indeed / Our shows are more than will; for still we prove / Much in our vows, but little in our love' (2.4.116–18). The fiction of her male identity allows Viola to generalize about male behaviour without arraigning Orsino directly.

What are we to make of this repeated configuration in the romantic comedies of the un-self-knowing man and the patiently instructive woman? It is as though Shakespeare is expressing, on behalf of his fellow males, a self-critical view. Men are impossible. They need help. Without denying them the ultimate position of superiority in the conventional hierarchy of a paternalistic culture, Shakespeare presents men as generally weak and helpless without the counsel and companionship of women. The attitude toward women is correspondingly one of gratitude and admiration, along with perhaps a grudging anxiety about male dependence. Young women enable men to grow up, to achieve a kind of emotional maturity and self-understanding that would be impossible without women's help. The women do so, moreover, in a way that minimizes the hazards of male transition from immaturity to maturity. By taking on the disguise of young men, as we see in ... Portia, Rosalind, and Viola, these young heroines erase the barrier of gender difference that many of Shakespeare's young men discover to be so daunting. Finding themselves in the congenial atmosphere of friendship seemingly between man and man, the young males in Shakespeare's romantic comedies begin to achieve insights and intimacies they have never known before. Once this loving friendship has ripened into a genuine mutuality, then the revelation of the woman's true sexual identity is no longer threatening. The play can end, presto-change-o, with the young woman (actually a boy actor) throwing off her/his disguise. . . .

Now, not all males in the romantic comedies are weak, to be sure. Even if the examples looked at thus far provide a compellingly consistent portrait of young men in love, they do not tell the whole story. Some males turn out to be remarkably self-assured, like Petruchio in *The Taming of the Shrew*. He has come from Verona 'to wive it wealthy in Padua;

/ If wealthily, then happily in Padua'. He is undaunted by the prospect of a shrewish wife, provided she be 'rich, / And very rich' (1.2.61–2, 74–5). The reported shrewishness of Kate is to him a challenge, not a potential hazard. Yet for all his professed interest in wealth as his uppermost consideration, Petruchio finds in Kate a worthy opponent, one whose wit deserves to be answered in kind. She in turn comes to find him more interesting by far than any of the other men she sees around her. She resists, of course, when he undertakes to tame her by putting on a grandiloquent display at their wedding and then dragging her off to his house before the wedding festivities are over. He deprives her of food and sleep, plays the tyrant with the servants, and then boasts in soliloquy of his success: 'He that knows better how to tame a shrew, / Now let him speak. 'Tis charity to show' (4.1.198–9). Whether the audience is to approve or disapprove of his behaviour as wooer and husband is today a celebratedly unsettled issue, but what can be said with confidence is that Petruchio knows what he is doing and that he succeeds in his own terms. 'I am he am born to tame you, Kate', he warns her at the start, 'And bring you from a wild Kate to a Kate / Conformable as other household Kates' (2.1.273–5). He never wavers from his plan. He justifies it as he goes along by comparing his method to the taming of a hawk (4.1.176–84). Kate learns eventually that she will be better off if she agrees with him that the sun is the moon when he says so, and that an old man may be transformed into a 'Young budding virgin' if he insists (4.5.1–48). In the concluding competition among husbands to see which of them is most contentedly married to an obedient wife, Petruchio wins hands down; Kate does as he bids her, to the point of throwing her own cap underfoot and then lecturing the other wives on the duty that every wife 'oweth to her husband', just like the duty that 'the subject owes the prince' (5.2.159–60). Perhaps, as often happens in stage productions today, she says this tongue in cheek, or even in such a way as to suggest that she has been relentlessly brainwashed, but at all events she has acceded to her husband's demands. He has won the argument. . . .

The raw conflict of Petruchio and Kate in *Taming* mellows appreciably in the famous war of words between Benedick and Beatrice in *Much Ado* [*About Nothing*]. Not that the exchanges are any less sharp and vehement. The difference is that a critical balance between the sexes is restored. Beatrice gives as good as she takes. During the evening revels of act 2, she trumps Benedick so resoundingly in their battle of wits that he is genuinely hurt; she has left him with the impression that she really does regard him as 'the Prince's jester, a very dull fool', whose only gift is 'in devising impossible slanders' (2.1.131–2). It is as though Shakespeare revisits the scene of *Taming* with a view to equalizing the contest. Beatrice is not asked to submit, nor does Benedick simply win. To the contrary, when Beatrice has something momentous to ask of him, he listens seriously and agrees to try. 'Kill Claudio', she demands of him, when Claudio has slandered her dear cousin Hero and has deserted Hero at the altar (4.1.288). Claudio is Benedick's friend and fellow officer. For Benedick to challenge Claudio and thus incur the enmity of him and of their commanding officer, Don Pedro, is a heavy burden indeed. Yet Benedick, unlike these men, has seen that something is seriously askew in the accusation brought against Hero by Don John, even if that accusation is backed by the seeming proof of what they saw at Hero's window on the night before her wedding. Benedick's own admirable scepticism, combined with his respect for Beatrice's insistent faith in Hero, gives to him a complex and mature view of human relationships that sets him apart from most of the other men in the play.

Overall, then, one can see in Shakespeare's romantic comedies a debate about men and women in the serious game of courtship. Just as George Lyman Kittredge has proposed a 'marriage group' in [English poet Geoffrey] Chaucer's *Canter-*

bury Tales, variously exploring the dimensions of romantic love from the tender to the sardonic, Shakespeare's romantic comedies look into many aspects of the question. If *Much Ado* represents something of an evolution in his thought about courtship, as compared with the earlier *Taming*, then perhaps Shakespeare is thinking his way through to a less paternalistic and less male-dominated idea about men and women. We need to be cautious about any such conclusion, since we are dealing with plays that stand by themselves as dramatic entertainments, but perhaps we have reason to expect that Shakespeare's thoughts about the relationships of the sexes should gain in complexity as he continues to revisit the subject.

Love and Courtship

Catherine Bates

*Catherine Bates is senior lecturer in the Department of English
and Comparative Literary Studies at the University of Warwick.
She has written extensively on Renaissance literature, including
such books as* The Rhetoric of Courtship in Elizabethan Language and Literature *(1992) and* Masculinity and the Hunt:
Wyatt to Spenser *(2013).*

*Catherine Bates contends in the following viewpoint that the
experience of passionate love and sexual desire transforms the
lovers in Shakespeare's romantic comedies. It throws them first
into chaos, from which they emerge on a clear trajectory toward
marriage. For Bates, marriage represents the control of sexuality
by law in that society may be ordered. Preceding this, however, is
a period of experimentation and confusion that is called courtship, a time and place where the rules are temporarily put on
hold. This period is the focus of Shakespeare's romantic comedies.*

Men and women meet, match, marry, and mate. This is
the eternal story which Shakespeare's comedies retell
again and again:

> Jack shall have Jill;
>
> Nought shall go ill:
>
> The man shall have his mare again, and all
> shall be well.
>
> (*A Midsummer Night's Dream*, 3.2.461–3) [1]

The details may vary considerably—and all is not always well—but in every comedy this basic formula remains the same. Sometimes men chase after women. Sometimes women chase after men. Often men pursue women who pursue other men who pursue women, giving us the mad merry-go-rounds of love we find in plays like *A Midsummer Night's Dream* or *The Two Gentlemen of Verona*. Frequently women turn themselves into men for a while, like Julia, Viola, or Rosalind. Less often men get themselves turned into women, like Falstaff, or, like Bottom, into beasts. But even if their actual shape or sex remains unchanged, everyone is in some way altered by love, transmuted into something rich and strange, or "metamorphis'd" like Proteus and Valentine (*Two Gentlemen of Verona*, 1.1.66, 2.1.30). The experience of passion changes everything: one's view of the world, of the beloved, even—or above all—one's own sense of self. Characters who, out of youth, inexperience, or disinclination had hitherto remained untouched by love suddenly find themselves caught up in the maelstrom of desire where everything is thrown into moral and emotional chaos before falling into a new *Gestalt* of socialized couples which represents the final (and, with luck, stable) product of this mysterious process of human natural selection.

Thankfully, the process does not go on forever. It may be protracted, prolonged, or excruciatingly postponed, but the period of courtship is never of infinite duration. It is always a fixed term, a brief spell during which individuals fall under the enchantment of love and bewitch each other with promises and vows. Courtship occupies a distinct period or interval, like the "midsummer madness" of *Twelfth Night* (3.4.56) or Rosalind's "holiday humor" in *As You Like It* (4.1.69). "Men are April when they woo," she pronounces, "December when they wed" (147–48). Even if it seems an eternity in the making, the whole thing is over in no time. If April's sweet showers make folk long for love, then the squally changeableness of the English spring—"Which now shows all the beauty of the sun, / And by and by a cloud takes all away" (*Two Gentlemen*, 1.3.86–87)—makes it the perfect season for blowing hot and cold and for suffering love's fervent hopes and cruel assaults. The lover has spring in his steps. As the Host cannily predicts of Fenton, the young and ultimately successful lover in *The Merry Wives of Windsor*, "he speaks holiday, he smells April and May—he will carry't, he will carry't—'tis in his buttons—he will carry't" (3.2.68–70).

Shakespeare's comedies are about courtship if they are about anything, but they are not, in this respect, either different or new. The timeless tale of boy meets girl was as hot a topic in the New Comedy of ancient Greece, the courtly romances of the Middle Ages, or the bawdy fabliau stories of folk tradition—all of which Shakespeare drew upon for his sources—as it continues to be to this day. Moreover, out of the whole vast spectrum of human relationships—social, economic, sexual, political, and familial—it has always been this highly specific relation between prospective marriage partners which has formed the staple of romantic comedy from the earliest times. Quite why this should be is a question worth pausing a moment to consider.

Whatever form it takes, a courtship narrative always charts some kind of development or progress. It moves its protagonists from one state of being to another that is clearly differentiated. The emphasis is on process—on the characters' passage through a sequence of normally well-recognized steps toward a desired, however distant, destination. "Your brother and my sister no sooner met but they look'd," Rosalind tells Orlando, "no sooner look'd but they lov'd; no sooner lov'd but they sigh'd; no sooner sigh'd but they ask'd one another the reason; no sooner knew the reason but they sought the remedy: and in these degrees have they made a pair of stairs to marriage" (*As You Like It*, 5.2.32–38). Few courtships are as blithely contracted as this one. Indeed, the romance between

Celia and Oliver is an exception, the rule in such cases being precisely those obstacles, delays, and misunderstandings which constitute the tortuous plots of most comedies of love. But, no matter how fraught or problematic a particular love affair, the courtship narrative traces a definite trajectory. Marriage may, as in a troubled play like *All's Well That Ends Well*, come near the beginning; or it may, as in *Love's Labour's Lost*, be postponed well beyond the conclusion: But in every case marriage is at least the promised end. No narrative structure is quite so teleological in its orientation, so heavily geared toward a final outcome.

Marriage—the end point to which courtship stories inevitably as if magnetically tend—is literary shorthand for the control of human sexuality by law. In its natural state human sexuality might look something like the world depicted in Ovid's *Metamorphoses*: a riot of rape, incest, homosexuality, bestiality, sex change, hermaphroditism, species pollution, and sexual perversion of every kind. In Ovid's text men have sex with gods, animals, objects, each other, and themselves—as indeed do women—and more than one character rejects the most primal taboos as artificial constraints upon sexual expression from which the animals are blissfully exempt. Yet it is such rules—the incest taboo, laws against consanguinity, the advisability of marriage outside the tribe, the establishment of polygamy or monogamy, and so forth—which wrestle to control this otherwise chaotic sexuality and bring it into some semblance of order. The laws regulating sexual conduct are second only to language in creating order out of chaos and in distinguishing men from the beasts. It is these laws which constitute human society—civilization, in a word—even if, as Freud believed, that society was as a consequence bound to be a repressive one. For these laws entail a massive reduction of all the infinite number of possible sexual permutations down to a single kind of allowable relation: one which specifies precisely who may have sex with whom, for what purpose, and when.

In Shakespeare's plays this relation is marriage and with it the no-nonsense heterosexual coupling as a result of which, as a reformed Benedick puts it, "the world must be peopled" (*Much Ado* [*About Nothing*], 2.3.242). Such sexual relations, licensed and endorsed by a host of social practices and solemnizations, are what make up civil society. Since the couple is the basic building block of the social group, matrimony celebrates not only the union of one particular happy couple but, more importantly, the absorption of that couple into the larger group as a whole. Ultimately the individual is subordinate to the group—something Shakespeare emphasizes in those plays which culminate not with one but with two (*Two Gentlemen, Twelfth Night*), three (*A Midsummer Night's Dream, The Taming of the Shrew*), or even four weddings (*As You Like It*, eventually *Love's Labour's Lost*).

At the end of courtship's arduous journey, the chaos finally settles. Couples submit to the laws of their society and take up their rightful positions as mature householders and sexually responsible adults—as parents, that is. As far as romantic comedy is concerned, this is a closed subject, as accepted and unarguable as the long-established relationships of the parents and guardians from which the younger generation both distance themselves and take their cue. Once couples have (with varying degrees of serenity) arrived on the marital shore, the curtain generally falls, for once licensed and regulated, sexuality ceases to be interesting. Of marriage romantic comedy has little or nothing to say, but of courtship it has to say a great deal. As William Congreve was to put it, courtship is to marriage as a very witty prologue to a very dull play.[2] For, although courtship leads like a pair of stairs to marriage, it still remains—structurally speaking—on the outside of that ordered state. And, if marriage represents sexuality regularized, then anything which precedes that state exists in an as yet unregularized state—one which calls to mind the preparatory, limbo state of the young initiate.

As just such a preliminary state—full of expectation but still awaiting final resolution—courtship is a quintessentially creative period, providing the amorphous and chaotic raw material from which order is soon to be drawn or upon which order will in due course be imposed. This is why literary courtships have traditionally opened out into a period of experiment and free play during which the rules are temporarily suspended, normal gender roles reversed, and hierarchies turned briefly upside down. It is also why the place for courtship is classically the forest, like that outside Athens in *A Midsummer Night's Dream*, or between Mantua and Milan in *Two Gentlemen of Verona*, or the Forest of Arden in *As You Like It*. For the forest is not only—as the "jolly greenwood"—an age-old locus for dalliance and fertility rituals, but more specifically (deriving from *foris*, "outside") a place that lies outside the jurisdiction of the city.[3] The forest does not necessarily specify an area of woodland but rather any wild or uncultivated place—like "the mountains and the barbarous caves, / Where manners ne'er were preached" to which Olivia threatens to banish the disorderly Sir Toby in *Twelfth Night* (4.1.48–49), or like the haunt of the outlaws in *Two Gentlemen of Verona* whose youthful crimes have thrust them "from the company of aweful men" (4.1.44). As a place which stands on the edges or outskirts of civilized society, and as refuge to all that society exiles and outcasts, the forest is a fitting place for those who have yet to take up their positions as fully fledged— that is to say, as married—citizens.

Courtship is a form of initiation rite which, in many societies, requires the parties to remove themselves to some second or "green" world from which they symbolically enact their reentry into the intitiated, norm-governed group.[4] And even where specifically forest retreats do not feature as such, most of Shakespeare's comedies echo this sense of movement to and from some mysterious or sinister realm, be it Portia's Belmont in *The Merchant of Venice* or Petruchio's country house in *The Taming of the Shrew*. With marriage, the couple is finally ushered through the door of regulated sexuality and, once the gate clangs shut, this marks for them a point of no return. But before that moment they effectively stand on the threshold, rather as the rowdy singers of epithalamia made their rough music on the threshold of the bridal chamber (*thalamos*). These singers stood "at the very chamber dore. . . in a large vtter roome," as George Puttenham puts it in *The Arte of English Poesie* (1588), there to play their drums and maracas (their loud and shrill music being designed, in the first instance, to drown out the screams of the virginal young bride upon "feeling the first forces of her stiffe and rigorous young man").[5] Comedies of love which center on courtship could be seen as extensions of this large outer room, and their actions could be characterized by the cacophonous clatter there expressed.

Uniquely positioned as a transitional phase and liminal state, courtship stands just on the outside of marriage and the ordering of sexuality that it represents. Courtship thus bears a curiously ambiguous—one could say, carnivalesque—relation to the law. As a general statement, this could be said of any period or society; however, courtship was in Shakespeare's day an area of particularly intense ambiguity. From the middle of the sixteenth century, both the church and state in England sought to clarify and pin down precisely what constituted matrimony in law. In 1597 and 1604 the church issued a series of canons which attempted to lay down unambiguous guidelines on the conduct of wedding services, the registering of marriages, and the issue of licenses and banns.[6] Up until then, however, and even for some time afterward, there remained a good deal of variety in local practice and accepted custom. The older form of spousals in which the two parties expressed their consent to marry in words of the present tense (*per verba de prasenti*), even if made in private or without witnesses, could still, strictly speaking, constitute a binding and indissoluble union. If courtship bore an ambiguous relation to the law at the best of times, then Shakespeare reflects on the very particular ambiguities that surrounded it in his own day, when the area was greyer than usual. Courtship could be defined simply as the period of wooing and winning that we find in most of the comedies. But it could also extend to that critical period between a betrothal and its formal solemnization in marriage (as with Claudio and Juliet in *Measure for Measure*); or even, more critically still, between the latter and its physical consummation in intercourse (as with Bertram and Helena in *All's Well*). In all these cases, we can see Shakespeare opening out that strange threshold state that stands just outside the law, testing contemporary definitions of courtship and seeing just how close he could get to that chamber door without quite passing through it.

Courtship narratives thus allow writers to explore and meditate upon the chaotic nature of human sexuality and the laws that set out to govern it. In the confrontation between something fluctuating, disorderly, and ultimately yielding, and something fixed, immutable, and stern one can see how the relation of sexuality to the law might easily correspond to some fairly obvious sexual stereotypes. (Not that women are always disorderly or men inclined to the law. The impact of love is as likely to make men's fancies "more giddy and unfirm, / More longing, wavering, sooner lost and worn, / Than women's are" as Orsino discovers in *Twelfth Night*, 2.4.33–35, while it is the women who, more often than not, keep a clear head.) In the course of most courtship narratives, a match of some kind is made between sexuality and the law. But, until it is, they remain uneasy sparring partners, batting power to and fro and furiously resisting closure—for all the world like one of Shakespeare's more skeptical and sharp-tongued courting couples. It is this critical relation between love and the law that is what courtship—or literary courtship, at any rate—is really about. And indeed it is this larger theme, rather than the particular relationship between this man or that woman, which makes courtship a topic so patient of repetition and a theme capable of such infinite variation.

Courtship's habitual scene is one of revelry and misrule and Shakespeare's comedies occupy a world of moral and emotional chaos in which the rules are temporarily put on hold. But they are not chaotic plays. On the contrary, in terms of formal construction they are among the most consummately ordered in the repertoire, giving us such miracles of plotting as *The Comedy of Errors*, based on the confusion of identical twins, or *The Merry Wives of Windsor*, in which multiple plots interlock with dazzling precision to enable wives to outwit lovers and husbands, servants to outwit masters, and daughters to outwit parents all in one go. Moral chaos seems no bar to formal perfection. Indeed, it is often at moments of the greatest moral dereliction that formal patternings emerge with the greatest flourish. In act 4 scene 3 of *Love's Labour's Lost*, the quadruple perjury of the menfolk—who, incapable of keeping their vows to abjure love, have all to a man succumbed to the charms of the French princess and her ladies—turns into a masterpiece of aesthetic design. The guilty confessions of the four men, unknowingly overheard by one another, allow Longaville to come forward and reproach Dumaine, the king to come forward and reproach the two of them in turn, and Berowne, who has been watching the whole "scene of fool'ry" from a tree (4.3.161), to come down and reproach all three, before being, in his turn, exposed by Costard, the clown. The moral high ground well and truly collapses and there are red faces all-round. Yet out of the morass of hypocrisy and shame comes a scene of exquisite craftsmanship, rather as, in an opera, the very worst treachery or disagreement can be expressed in music of the most harmonious kind.

Notes

1. All references to Shakespeare are to *The Riverside Shakespeare,* 2nd edn, ed. G. Blakemore Evans et al. (Boston and New York: Houghton Mifflin Company, 1997).

2. William Congreve, *The Old Bachelor* (1693), 5.I.388, in *The Complete Plays of William Congreve*, ed. Herbert Davis (Chicago: University of Chicago Press, 1967), p. 107.

3. For some examples of amorous "greenwood" songs, see John Stevens, *Music and Poetry in the Early Tudor Court* (London: Methuen, 1961), pp. 338, 400, 408, 410.

4. For a particularly interesting discussion of this, see Harry Berger, *Second World and Green World: Studies in Renaissance Fiction-Making* (Berkeley: University of California Press, 1988).

5. George Puttenham, *The Arte of English Poesie*, ed. G.D. Willcock and Alice Walker (Cambridge: Cambridge University Press, 1936), p. 51.

6. See Martin Ingram, *Church Courts, Sex and Marriage in England, 1570–1640*, (Cambridge: Cambridge University Press, 1987).

Sexual Tension in *The Taming of the Shrew*

Maurice Charney

A prolific writer and teacher of Shakespeare, Maurice Charney is professor emeritus of English at Rutgers University. Among his books on Shakespeare are All of Shakespeare *(1993) and* Shakespeare's Villains *(2011). He is also a past president of the Shakespeare Association of America.*

In The Taming of the Shrew, *Shakespeare gives us two intelligent, strong-willed characters who make their way to love and marriage the hard way—through the teasing, taunting, and arguing sometimes called "wit combat." Maurice Charney in the following viewpoint observes that, along the way, their banter includes plenty of sexual innuendo and punning. He notes that, though Petruchio is the apparent "winner" of this taming contest, he too undergoes a process of change by the end, becoming tame himself in the newfound harmony of love.*

The most problematic of the comedies—at least in relation to contemporary criticism—is undoubtedly *The Taming of the Shrew*. It is clearly misogynistic, attacked by many (but not all) feminist critics of Shakespeare, yet it also may be considered a conspicuously loving play, with Kate and Petruchio (like Beatrice and Benedick) admirably suited for each other. Can these two opposing points of view be reconciled? Obviously not, but there is a sense that Petruchio has met his match, as is evident in John Fletcher's sequel, *The Woman's Prize, or The Tamer Tamed* (1611), which reverses the roles of Petruchio and Kate. Fletcher and Shakespeare worked together for the King's Men company and may have collaborated on *The Two Noble Kinsmen*. Fletcher must have known Shakespeare's play, so his play functions as a kind of commentary on it.

We get hints of the other side of the Petruchio action throughout the play, but especially when Gremio says "I warrant him, Petruchio is Kated" (3.2.245). Petruchio is a fortune hunter, like Bassanio in *The Merchant of Venice*, but that doesn't mean he gets exactly what he is looking for—a rich marriage. Petruchio gets more than he bargains for, as does Bassanio. If we take *The Merchant of Venice* as parallel to *The Taming of the Shrew*, it was no part of Bassanio's intention to fall in love with Portia. That is pure lagniappe.

Spontaneous Wit Combat

The first wooing scene (2.1) between Kate and Petruchio is a case in point. It is patently a wit combat, with Petruchio not so dominant as he seems to think. Kate gives as good as she gets, and the dialogue is not only witty but also provokingly sexual. Petruchio and Kate are clearly the only intelligent characters in the play. Notice how spontaneously and effortlessly the love game unfolds. Petruchio's plan, as he explains it to Baptista, Kate's father, does not exactly forecast the way things will turn out:

I am as peremptory as she proud-minded.

And where two raging fires meet together

They do consume the thing that feeds their
fury.

In his soliloquy right before Kate enters, Petruchio again enunciates his plan, as if it is necessary to keep the audience (as well as himself) informed of how things are expected to go in order to rule out randomness. Petruchio seems to be reassuring himself and assuaging his fears with his soliloquies:

Say that she rail, why then I'll tell her plain

She sings as sweetly as a nightingale.

Say that she frown, I'll say she looks as clear

As morning roses newly washed with dew.

But Kate is not so simple as to be taken in by all these mechanistic contraries. She definitely has a mind of her own.

Sexual Wordplay

In the lively scene Kate is full of insulting puns and double entendres. She calls Petruchio a "movable" (197), or piece of furniture, a "joint stool" (198), or a stool made by a joiner or carpenter, to which Petruchio replies: "Thou hast hit it; come sit on me" (198). The next two lines are made to match each other as witty ripostes:

KATE: Asses are made to bear and so are you.

PETRUCHIO: Women are made to bear and so are you.

(199–200)

The whole scene reverberates with clashing rejoinders, ending with an obscene reference to the wasp and its sting. Petruchio calls her an angry "wasp" (209) and Kate replies: "If I be waspish, best beware my sting" (210).

This begins a chain of associations:

PETRUCHIO: Who knows not where a wasp does wear his sting?

In his tail.

KATE: In his tongue.

PETRUCHIO: Whose tongue?

KATE: Yours, if you talk of tales, and so farewell.

> PETRUCHIO: What, with my tongue in your
> tail?
>
> (213–16)

This is grossly sexual, as is his reply to Kate's question:

> KATE: What is your crest? A coxcomb?
>
> PETRUCHIO: A combless cock, so Kate will be
> my hen.
>
> (223–24)

The sexual references and the nonstop punning energize the scene. Kate and Petruchio obviously enjoy each other's company, and this scene shows her as not just shrewd, curst, froward, and toward, as she is repeatedly described in the play, but also witty, sportive, intelligent, and gamesome—not unlike Petruchio at his best. There is not a little irony in Petruchio's comment: "in a twink [=twinkling] she won me to her love" (303). His last line before he exits is "kiss me, Kate" (317), which echoes like a refrain in the play. Why does he want to kiss her if he is only after her dowry?

The Implications of Taming

What does "taming" mean in this play? Obviously, one thing to Petruchio and another to Kate. Yet there is also a sense that Petruchio doesn't understand the implications of taming, just as Christopher Sly in the Induction is not really tamed by the rich lord who transforms him from a drunken tinker, or [Nick] Bottom the Weaver is not really tamed by Titania, the Queen of the Fairies, in *A Midsummer Night's Dream*. He is only "translated." Perhaps if "taming" is understood as a histrionic word, then some of the taming backfires on Petruchio, as Kate becomes more and more masterful at the love game.

Petruchio's long soliloquy in act 4, scene 1 is awfully naive about Kate as we perceive her in the play. She is not at all as he imagines her:

Samantha Spiro as Kate and Simon Paisley Day as Petruchio in William Shakespeare's The Taming of the Shrew, *directed by Toby Frow at Shakespeare's Globe Theatre in London in 2012.* © Robbie Jack/Robbie Jack/Corbis.

> Another way I have to man my haggard
> [=wild hawk captured after maturity],
>
> To make her come and know her keeper's
> call,
>
> That is, to watch her as we watch these kites
>
> That bate and beat and will not be obedient.
>
> (187–90)

Petruchio wishes that it will all be as simple as he projects, but he himself graciously undergoes all of the instructional torments intended for Kate, including not eating, not sleeping, and not participating in the pleasures of the wedding night. He emerges from the ordeal as hungry and sleepless and deprived of affection and sex as Kate. He is tamed too and different from the blustering fortune hunter at the beginning of the play.

At the end of act 5, scene 1, Kate and Petruchio are seen as a loving couple, but still politely brawling like Benedick and

Beatrice in *Much Ado* [*About Nothing*]. When Petruchio enunciates his favorite verbal formula, "kiss me, Kate" (142), Kate objects: "What, in the midst of the street?" (143), but yields tenderly anyhow: "Nay, I will give thee a kiss. Now pray thee, love, stay" (148). Notice that she addresses her husband as "love." Petruchio is delighted:

> Is not this well? Come, my sweet Kate.
>
> Better once than never, for never too late.
>
> (149–50)

He needs to have his loving relation to his wife demonstrated over and over again.

Playing the Good Wife

This leads directly into the last scene of the play, with the wager among the men and Kate's groveling oration about a wife's duty to her husband, ideas already expressed in *The Comedy of Errors*. This speech has really annoyed feminist critics, but in context it is something different from its literal meaning. It is not ironic but sportive. Kate knows finally how to play the good wife, and the wager is almost perfectly suited for Petruchio and Kate to demonstrate their connubial harmony and to win a lot of loot. Kate speaks of wifely obedience as if she were reading a speech from a contemporary marriage manual: a husband "craves no other tribute at thy hands / But love, fair looks, and true obedience" (5.2.152–53). Kate offers the physiological argument about women's bodies in relation to women's temperament, as if it weren't one of the most tedious and specious of clichés:

> Why are our bodies soft and weak and
> smooth,
>
> Unapt to toil and trouble in the world,
>
> But that our soft conditions [=qualities] and
> our hearts

Should well agree with our external parts?

(165–68)

Never in the play has it seemed that Kate's body is "soft and weak and smooth" or that she depends on her "soft conditions." This is all a convenient gamester's fiction.

The bet is won and Petruchio says again, this time with real pride and astonishment: "Why, there's a wench! Come on and kiss me, Kate" (180). His last speech goes even further in his admiration for his new wife: "Come, Kate, we'll to bed" (184). This doesn't mean, as critics trained in motive-hunting might say, that the marriage has not yet been consummated, but it does indicate that Petruchio, the fortune hunter, thinks he has gotten a much better deal than he bargained for, and a wife that puts Kate's prim sister, Bianca, to shame, as well as Hortensio's much-labored-for Widow. *The Taming of the Shrew* is after all only a play-within-a-play, put on for Christopher Sly's benefit and meant to convince him of the magical nature of the world that now opens up for him. I don't think we are meant to take the presented play too literally and to substitute what the characters say for what they mean. Both Christopher Sly's play and the play of Petruchio and Kate are alike in being full of games and deceptions. Petruchio and Kate emerge from their extensive love combat with new understandings of reality. They are strongly attracted to each other, have fun in each other's company, and wind up as an affectionate married couple. No one could have predicted this conclusion at the beginning of the play.

The Power of Passionate Love in *A Midsummer Night's Dream*

Alexander Leggatt

Now professor emeritus of English at University College, University of Toronto, Alexander Leggatt has published extensively on Shakespearean topics. He is editor of The Cambridge Companion to Shakespearean Comedy *(2002) and author of* Introduction to English Renaissance Comedy *(1999).*

According to Alexander Leggatt in the following viewpoint, Shakespeare portrays passionate love as a force that turns the characters smitten by turning them into frantic and irrational creatures. All the lovers in the play are subject to their own foolish, limited perspective on love, epitomized by the ridiculous love encounter between the fairy queen Titania and the weaver Nick Bottom. Though the love relationships become confusing, and some quite contentious, in the end harmony is restored, even though the lovers cannot understand how or why. Shakespeare depicts passionate love as a transforming power beyond the control or comprehension of mere mortals.

When Titania meets [Nick] Bottom in the wood near Athens, we see a fairy confronting a mortal, and finding him more wonderful than he finds her. For Titania, Bottom—ass's head and all—is an object of rare grace and beauty; for Bottom, the queen of the fairies is a lady he has just met, who is behaving a bit strangely, but who can be engaged in ordinary, natural conversation:

TITANIA: I pray thee, gentle mortal, sing again.

Mine ear is much enamoured of thy note;

So is mine eye enthralled to thy shape;

And thy fair virtue's force perforce doth
move me,

On the first view, to say, to swear, I love
thee.

BOTTOM: Methinks, mistress, you should have
little reason for that. And yet, to say the
truth, reason and love keep little company
together now-a-days. The more the pity that
some honest neighbours will not make them
friends. Nay, I can gleek upon occasion.

TITANIA: Thou art as wise as thou art beautiful.

(III. i. 125–35)

This is, by now, a familiar effect. Behind the sharply contrasted voices are two utterly different kinds of understanding,
and each one comically dislocates the other. Titania's love is
addressed to a hearer who uses it simply as the occasion for a
bit of cheerful philosophizing. And the philosophy, in turn, is
wasted on the listener. It is all very well for Bottom to chatter
away about reason and love; he has the detachment of the to-
tally immune. But Titania is caught up in the experience of
which Bottom is only a detached observer, and, ironically, his
cool philosophy only gives her one more reason for adoring
him. . . .

Innocence with Dignity

Bottom and Titania present the play's most striking image, a
pairing of disparate beings whose contact only emphasizes the
difference between them. It looks for a moment as though the
barrier between the mortal and immortal worlds has fallen;

but on inspection, the barrier proves as secure as ever. Instead of a fusion of worlds we are given a series of neat comic contrasts. And throughout the play, we see four different groups of characters—the lovers, the clowns, the older Athenians and the fairies—each group preoccupied with its own limited problems, and largely unaware of the others. When they make contact, it is usually to emphasize the difference between them. All are to some degree innocent, though (as we shall see) the degree of innocence varies. But the play weaves them all together. Each group, so self-absorbed, is seen in a larger context, which provides comic perspective. Each in turn provides a similar context for the others, and if here and there we feel tempted to take sides, we can never do so for very long; for while each group has its own folly, it has its own integrity as well, and its own special, coherent view of life.

We are reminded throughout of the workings of perception, and in particular of the way we depend on perception—special and limited though it may be—for our awareness of the world. . . .

The conflict between Hermia and her father, for example, is seen as a difference of perception:

HERMIA: I would my father look'd but with my eyes.

THESEUS: Rather your eyes must with his judgment look.

(I. i. 56–7)

When Hermia and Egeus look at Lysander, they see two different people, for she sees with the eyes of love, he with the eyes of cantankerous old age, obsessed with its own authority.

The Courage and Integrity of Love

In the opening scene, the lovers are on the defensive, set against the hostility of Egeus and the more restrained, regretful opposition of Theseus. Egeus's lecture to Lysander presents love from an outsider's point of view, as trivial, deceitful and disruptive of good order:

Thou hast by moonlight at her window
sung,

With feigning voice, verses of feigning love,

And stol'n the impression of her fantasy

With bracelets of thy hair, rings, gawds, conceits,

Knacks, trifles, nosegays, sweetmeats, messengers

Of strong prevailment in unhardened youth;

With cunning hast thou filch'd my
daughter's heart;

Turn'd her obedience, which is due to me,

To stubborn harshness.

(I. i. 30–8)

Against this crabbed but concrete and detailed attack, Hermia's defence, though deeply felt, is inarticulate: 'I know not by what power I am made bold . . .' (I. i. 59). But it suggests that love is a force bearing down all normal authority, and arming the lover with strength to meet the hostility of the outside world. It gives Hermia the courage to defy her father and the Duke in open court, and to accept the pains and trials love must always bear:

If then true lovers have been ever cross'd,

It stands as an edict in destiny.

Then let us teach our trial patience,

Because it is a customary cross . . .

(I. i. 150–3)

Love, to the outsider, appears foolish; but in accepting its demands the lovers acquire their own kind of integrity.

Their vision of the world is transformed. In Hermia's words,

Before the time I did Lysander see,

Seem'd Athens as a paradise to me.

O, then, what graces in my love do dwell,

That he hath turn'd a heaven into a hell!

(I. i. 204–7)

And for Helena the forest is similarly transformed by the presence of Demetrius:

It is not night when I do see your face,

Therefore I think I am not in the night,

Nor doth this wood lack worlds of company,

For you, in my respect, are all the world.

(II. i. 221–4)

But there is also something comically irrational in these transformations. In particular, the lover's perception of his beloved, and his judgement of her, are peculiar and inexplicable, so much so that even to the lovers themselves love seems blind. As [Helena] says of Demetrius,

And as he errs, doting on Hermia's eyes,

So I, admiring of his qualities.

Things base and vile, holding no quantity,

Love can transpose to form and dignity.

Love looks not with the eyes, but with the
mind;

And therefore is wing'd Cupid painted blind.

Nor hath Love's mind of any judgment
taste;

Wings and no eyes figure unheedy haste;

And therefore is Love said to be a child,

Because in choice he is so oft beguil'd.

(I. i. 230–9)

It is not Hermia's beauty that inspires Demetrius's love: 'Through Athens I am thought as fair as she' (I. i. 227). It is rather that love imposes its own peculiar kind of vision, which renders any other opinion—including that of common sense—irrelevant. How far Helena's own senses have been taken over by this vision may be judged by her decision to betray her friend to Demetrius:

for this intelligence

If I have thanks, it is a dear expense.

But herein mean I to enrich my pain,

To have his sight thither and back again.

(I. i. 248–51)

In love, the mere sight of the beloved acquires an importance that by any normal standards would be absurd.

Conventional Language of Love

The lovers may find each other's choices inexplicable, but at least they share the same kind of experience: They are in the grip of a power that renders choice and will meaningless. One sign of this is that the lovers lack the conscious awareness of convention that distinguishes Berowne and the ladies in *Love's Labour's Lost*. They slip naturally into a stylized manner of speech:

An illustration of A Midsummer Night's Dream. © Titania Awakes, Surrounded by Attendant Fairies, clinging rapturously to Bottom, still wearing the Ass's Head, 1793–4, Fuseli, Henry (Fuseli, Johann Heinrich) (1741–1825)/Kunsthaus, Zurich, Switzerland/ The Bridgeman Art Library.

LYSANDER: Ay me! For aught that I could ever read,

Gould ever learn by tale or history,

The course of true love never did run smooth;

But either it was different in blood—

HERMIA: O cross! too high to be enthrall'd to
low.

LYSANDER: Or else ingraffed in respect of
years—

HERMIA: O spite! too old to be engag'd to
young.

LYSANDER: Or else it stood upon the choice of
friends—

HERMIA: O hell! to choose love by another's
eyes.

(I. i. 132–40)

There is something ceremonial about this passage, with its li-
turgical responses, and like all ceremonies it presents the individual experience as part of a larger and more general pattern.
The individual can assert his independence of this process
only by showing his awareness of it and standing partly outside it, as Berowne attempts to do. But Lysander and Hermia
surrender to the ceremony, taking its patterned language as a
normal mode of speech. Later in the same scene, Hermia falls
into a playful, teasing style as she swears to meet Lysander:

I swear to thee by Cupid's strongest bow,

By his best arrow with the golden head,

By the simplicity of Venus' doves,

By that which knitteth souls and prospers
loves,

And by that fire which burn'd the Carthage
Queen,

When the false Troyan under sail was seen,

By all the vows that ever men have broke,

In number more than ever women spoke,

In that same place thou hast appointed me,

Tomorrow truly will I meet with thee.

(I. i. 169–78)

There is, this time, a deliberate playfulness in the way the literary allusions pile up, as she teases her lover by comparing male infidelity and female faith. But the speech flows swiftly and easily, and the joking does no damage; she can afford to toy with her love because she is so sure of it. (There is a similar quality in their affectionate banter about sleeping arrangements in the forest—II. ii. 39–61.) The joking with love is not that of an outsider exposing its weakness, but that of an insider confident of its strength, and feeling that strength by subjecting it to a little harmless teasing. And once again, the character herself gives no indication that this manner of speech is anything other than perfectly natural.

The exchange on the course of true love is slow and brooding; Hermia's speech, swift and gay. The common factor is an air of literary artifice that sets the lovers' experience apart as something special; and throughout the play the range of expression achieved within this framework of artifice is remarkable. We see this, for example, when Lysander awakes to find himself in love with Helena:

The will of man is by his reason sway'd,

And reason says you are the worthier maid.

Things growing are not ripe until their season;

So I, being young, till now ripe not to reason;

And touching now the point of human skill,

Reason becomes the marshal to my will,

And leads me to your eyes, where I o'erlook

Love's stories, written in Love's richest book.

HELENA: Wherefore was I to this keen mockery born?

When at your hands did I deserve this
scorn?

Is't not enough, is't not enough, young man,

That I did never, no, nor never can,

Deserve a sweet look from Demetrius' eye,

But you must flout my insufficiency?

Good troth, you do me wrong, good sooth,
you do,

In such disdainful manner me to woo.

(II. ii. 115–30)

Lysander's speech is formal, solemn, sententious—and thoroughly dislocated by its context. He describes his love as natural and reasonable, but we know it is purely arbitrary. Here
the character's unawareness of his own dependence on convention becomes sharply comic. Helena's irritable retort gives
us, by contrast, the sound of a natural speaking voice; there is
a striking difference in tone and pace. And yet it too is in
rhyming couplets: Her seemingly natural utterance is still contained within the framework of a convention; her anger, no
less than his infatuation, is part of the larger, dance-like pattern in which all four lovers are unconsciously moving.

Ironic Detachment

The lovers see their experiences in the forest as chaotic; but
for the audience the disorder, like the disorder of a Feydeau
farce, is neatly organized, giving us pleasure where it gives
them pain. When Hermia accuses Demetrius of killing

Lysander, the patterned language and the rhymed couplets cool the emotional impact the scene might have had (III. ii. 43–81). Over and over, the violence of the ideas is lightened by jingling rhythm and rhyme: 'I'll follow thee, and make a heaven of hell, / To die upon the hand I love so well' (II. i. 243–4). It is not so much that, as Enid Welsford suggests, 'the harmony and grace of the action would have been spoilt by convincing passion'; it is more that the manner of the action in itself ensures that the passion is convincing only to the characters. They lash out frantically at each other, but the audience is too far away to share in their feelings. Our detachment is aided by the presence of Puck and Oberon, acting as an onstage audience and providing a comic perspective. What is serious and painful to the lovers is simply a 'fond pageant' of mortal foolishness to the watchers (III. ii. 144). Puck in particular regards the whole affair as a show put on for his amusement (and incidentally if we can remember this in the final scene it adds a level of irony to the lovers' laughter as they watch Pyramus and Thisbe: They too, not so long ago, amused an audience with antics that they thought were serious). The irony is compounded when the lovers indignantly accuse each other of playing games with serious feelings: 'Wink at each other; hold the sweet jest up; / This sport, well carried, shall be chronicled' (III. ii. 239–40). Helena's accusation is very close to the truth—except that it should be directed at the audience.

But our feelings are subtly managed here: There are two watchers—Puck, with his delight in chaos, and Oberon, who wishes to bring chaos to an end. We share in both these attitudes. When Helena recalls her childhood friendship with Hermia, the rhyme slips away and it becomes a little easier to take the characters' feelings seriously (III. ii. 195–219). From this point on, the formality breaks down into undignified, farcical squabbling, with physical knockabout and coarse insults—relieved, on one occasion, by a surprisingly quiet and dignified speech from Helena:

Good Hermia, do not be so bitter with me.

I evermore did love you, Hermia,

Did ever keep your counsel, never wrong'd
you;

Save that, in love unto Demetrius,

I told him of your stealth unto this
wood. . . .

And now, so you will let me quiet go,

To Athens I will bear my folly back,

And follow you no further.

(III. ii. 306–16)

While still enjoying the confusion, we are beginning to feel that it had better stop soon. And Oberon and Puck see that it does.

A Ritual Sense of Life

But we are kept at a distance from the lovers' final union, no less than from their suffering. In the last stages of their ordeal, formality returns and is further heightened: A variety of rhymed verse forms accumulates as, one by one, the lovers enter and fall asleep. Their individuality is at a particularly low ebb, as Puck controls them more directly than ever, even to the point of assuming the men's voices (III. ii. 396–463). The final harmony he creates for them, like the earlier confusion, is seen as the working out of a dance pattern; and more than that, it is the fulfillment of a ritual sense of life, embodied in homely clichés:

And the country proverb known,

That every man should take his own,

In your waking shall be shown.

> Jack shall have Jill;
>
> Nought shall go ill;
>
> The man shall have his mare again, and all
> shall be well.
>
> (III. ii. 458–63)

Similarly, Theseus sees their coupling in terms of sport and pastime—'No doubt they rose up early to observe / The rite of May' (IV. i. 129–30)—and as a fulfillment of nature's most basic impulse: 'Good morrow, friends. Saint Valentine is past; / Begin these wood-birds but to couple now?' (IV. i. 136–7). The presence, and the comments, of other characters provide the awareness of convention that the lovers themselves lack, being too caught up in their own experiences. We see love's perceptions as special and limited, and the lovers themselves as lacking in full self-awareness. The magic flower is applied, significantly, to the eye; just as significantly, it is applied while the lover is asleep. And even the final harmony of love, when seen through the homely analogies of Puck and Theseus, is satisfying but nothing to get ecstatic about: 'The man shall have his mare again, and all shall be well' sounds like the voice of a parent comforting a child who has been making a great fuss about nothing. It is certainly not how the lovers themselves would have put it. At the same time, however, we recognize that the lovers *have got* what they want: The law of Athens, so formidable in the first scene, is swept away to accommodate them, and Egeus is reduced to spluttering impotence. In our final attitude to the lovers, there is respect as well as amused detachment.

Sexual Anxiety in *Much Ado About Nothing*

Carol Thomas Neely

Scholar Carol Thomas Neely is professor emerita of English at the University of Illinois at Urbana-Champaign. She is coeditor of The Woman's Part: Feminist Criticism of Shakespeare *(1983) and author of* Distracted Subjects: Madness and Gender in Shakespeare and Early Modern Culture *(2004).*

Carol Thomas Neely argues in the following viewpoint that many of Shakespeare's romantic comedies share a common moment—the moment when potential marriages are broken off due to a discovered impediment. She calls these moments "broken nuptials" and finds the clearest example in Much Ado About Nothing. *One function of the broken nuptial is to reveal the deep, latent sexual anxieties and fear of marriage shared by many characters. The lovers typically fear sexual betrayal and infidelity, as well as the loss of control, freedom, and individuality that comes with marriage.*

In Shakespearean comedy, if wooing is to lead to a wedding ceremony and consummation of the marriage, separation from family and friends must occur, misogyny must be exorcised, romantic idealizing affection must be experienced and qualified, and sexual desire must be acknowledged and controlled. Only then can romance and desire be reconciled in a formal social ceremony. Resistance to marriage is variously manifested and mitigated and is different for men and women. Women often bear a double burden. Once released from their own fears, usually through the actions of other women, they must dispel men's resistance and transform men's emotions. Various impediments to the comic project are revealed and removed by the irregular nuptials in three early comedies: Kate's opposition to romantic affection in *The Taming of the Shrew*, which is transformed by Petruchio; the men's vacillation between misogyny and romanticism in *Love's Labour's Lost*, which is mocked and countered by the ladies; and the capricious, aggressive action of desire in *A Midsummer Night's Dream*, which is experienced and manipulated by both men and women and transforms them. . . .

Anxieties About Romantic Love

Much Ado About Nothing contains the most clear-cut example of broken nuptials—Claudio's interruption of his wedding ceremony to accuse Hero of infidelity. Poised at the center of the comedies, the play looks both backward and forward.[1] Its tensions and its poise are achieved by the interactions of its two plots, its two couples. None of the other comedies includes two such sharply contrasted, subtly interrelated, and equally important couples. While, despite some uneasiness about the issue, critics are generally in agreement that the Claudio/Hero story is the main plot and the Beatrice/Benedick story the subplot, they also concur that the subplot couple is rhetorically richer, dramatically more interesting, and psychologically more complex than the main plot couple.[2] . . .

In the Claudio/Hero plot, the anxieties and risks underlying the conventions of romantic love are expressed and contained by the broken nuptials, Hero's vilification and mock death, and Claudio's penitence and acceptance of a substitute bride, motifs that are developed further in *All's Well* [*That Ends Well*], *Measure for Measure*, and the late romances. In the Beatrice/Benedick plot, the mutual mockery, double gulling, and Benedick's acceptance of Beatrice's command to "Kill Claudio" function, as do the mockery, trickery, parody, and tamings of the festive comedies, to break down resistance and to release desire and affection. The Beatrice/Benedick plot protects the Hero/Claudio plot by ventilating and displacing it and by transforming its romance elements. In turn, the impasse of the Hero/Claudio plot generates movement in the Beatrice/Benedick plot and, by permitting the witty couple the expression of romantic affection, initiates the transformation of their "merry wars" into a witty truce.[3]...

Sexual Teasing

The two plots are played out against a backdrop of patriarchal authority, which is protected by the extensive bawdy, especially the cuckoldry jokes, and contained by the ineffectuality of the men's exercise of power, especially when exaggerated in the Dogberry subplot. The play's lighthearted, witty bawdy expresses and mutes sexual anxieties; it turns them into a communal joke and provides comic release and relief in specific ways. It manifests sexuality as the central component of marriage and emphasizes male power and female weakness. Its clever, inventive innuendo emphasizes the anatomical "fit" between the sexes: "Give us the swords; we have bucklers of our own" (V.ii.19).

The bawdy persistently views sex as a male assault on women. Men "board" (II.i.138) women, "put in the pikes" (V.ii.20), and women cheerfully resign themselves to being "made heavier ... by the weight of a man," and "stuff'd" (III.iv.26, 62–63). The women counterattack by mocking the virility that threatens them: the "blunt foils" (V.ii.14), "short horns" (II.i.22), and "fine little" wit (V.i.161) of the men. They do not, however, see their own sexuality as a weapon. They joke about female "lightness" (III.iv.36, 43, 45) to warn each other against it, not to threaten men; even the term itself identifies women with weakness rather than strength.

But women's proverbial "lightness" is also a source of power. Women fear submission to men's aggressive sexual power. Men, likewise perceiving sexuality as power over women, fear its loss through female betrayal. They defend themselves against betrayal in three ways: They deny its possibility through idealization, anticipate it through misogyny, or transform it, through the motif of cuckoldry, into an emblem of male virility. . . .

Verbal Warfare

The witty verbal skirmishes comprising Beatrice's and Benedick's "merry wars" explicitly express the anxieties about loss of power through sexuality, love, and marriage that lie beneath Claudio's and Hero's silent romanticism. Their verbal wars fill up the silence of the Hero/Claudio plot and reveal the fundamental asymmetry of the battle of the sexes. Benedick expressly equates loving with humiliation and loss of potency; he imagines it as a castrating torture: "Prove that ever I lose more blood with love than I will get again with drinking, pick out mine eyes with a ballad maker's pen and hang me up at the door of a brothel house for the sign of blind Cupid" (I.i.243–47). He likewise fears being separated from his friends by marriage and loss of status with them if he must "sigh away Sundays" or, feminized, "turn spit" like Hercules (I.i.196; II.i.244). He defends himself against a fall into love and marriage and against fears of female betrayal by distrust of women—"I will do myself the right to trust none" (I.i.237). Distrust, coupled with the claim that all women dote on him, allows him to profess virility without putting it to the proof. Mocking Claudio's romantic idealization, he is similarly protected by misogyny; the parallel function of the two poses is evident in Benedick's admission that, could he find an ideal woman, he would abandon the pose: "But till all graces be in one woman, one woman shall not come in my grace" (II.iii.27–29). As he continues his description of the ideal woman, it is clear that she, like Claudio's Hero, meets the conventional prescriptions for a suitably accomplished and submissive wife:

"Rich she shall be, that's certain; wise, or I'll none; virtuous, or I'll never cheapen her; fair, or I'll never look on her; mild, or come not near me; noble, or not I for an angel; of good discourse, an excellent musician" (II.iii.29–33). Benedick's misogyny puts him in a position of unchallengeable power; his wit is consistently belligerent, protective, and self-aggrandizing. But his bawdy incorporates, as romantic rhetoric does not, the aggressiveness and urgency of desire even while defending against it.

Self-Deprecating Wit

Instead of defensively asserting power and certainty, Beatrice's sallies often directly reveal weakness and ambivalence; her wit, in contrast to Benedick's, is consistently self-deprecating. Her mockery of marriage and men poignantly reveals her desire for both. The fear of and desire for women's roles that generate her merry mask are suggested in her description of her birth and her mother's response to it—"No, sure, my lord, my mother cried; but then there was a star danced, and under that was I born" (II.i.322–23)—and in Leonato's similarly paradoxical description of her—"She hath often dreamt of unhappiness and waked herself with laughing" (II.i.333). Her repartee, like that of the others, embodies anxiety about being unmarried, as it does about being married: "So, by being too curst, God will send you no horns" (II.i.23). She does not mock Hero's marriage plans as Benedick does Claudio's but only urges her to marry a man who pleases her. Hero's engagement does not engender smug self-satisfaction in her but a sense of isolation: "Thus goes everyone to the world but I, and I am sunburnt. I may sit in a corner and cry 'Heigh-ho for a husband!'" (II.i.306–08). Even her allusion to living "as merry as the day is long" in heaven "where the bachelors sit" shows her desire to continue to share equally in easy male camaraderie rather than a desire to remain single (II.i.45–47).[4]

Pride and Fear of Marriage

Beatrice's ambivalence about marriage is rooted in her fear of the social and sexual power it grants to men. Her bawdy jests manifest both her desire for Benedick and her fear of the potential control over her which her desire gives him. In the first scene it is she who quickly shifts the play's focus from Claudio's deeds of war to Benedick's deeds of love. She refers to him as "Signior Mountanto," suggestively initiates dialogue by asking, "Is it possible Disdain should die while she hath such food to feed it as Signior Benedick?" (I.i.29,117), and from behind the safety of her mask admits to Benedick (of him)—"I would he had boarded me" (II.i.137). But her jesting about the unsuitability of husbands with beards and those without them both mocks Benedick's beard and reveals her ambivalent attitude toward virility: "He that hath a beard is more than a youth, and he that hath no beard is less than a man; and he that is more than a youth is not for me, and he that is less than a man, I am not for him" (II.i.34–37). Because she is apprehensive about the social and sexual submission demanded of women in marriage and wary of men's volatile mixture of earthly frailty with arrogant authority, Beatrice does not want a husband:

> Till God make men of some other metal than earth. Would it not grieve a woman to be overmastered with a piece of valiant dust? To make an account of her life to a clod of wayward marl? No, uncle, I'll none. Adam's sons are my brethren, and truly I hold it a sin to match in my kindred. [II.i.56–61]

Neither hating nor idealizing men, she does not wish to exchange kinship with them for submission to them. Given the play's dominant metaphor of sex as a male assault, the subordination demanded of Renaissance women in marriage, and the valiant cloddishness of many of the men in the comedies, Beatrice's fear of being "overmastered" seems judicious. But her anxieties, like Benedick's, grow out of pride and fear of risk as well as out of justified wariness.

Beatrice and Benedick, both mockers of love, cannot dispel these anxieties or admit to love without intervention. The asymmetrical gullings perpetrated by their friends (the "only love-gods" in this play, II.i.372) resemble the ceremonies mocking men and the attacks on female recalcitrance already examined. These garrulous deceits follow upon and displace Hero and Claudio's silent engagement and confront anxieties there left unspoken. As male and female anxieties are different, the two deceits are contrasting. The men gently mock Benedick's witty misogyny while nurturing his ego. Their gentle ribbing of Benedick's "contemptible spirit" is tempered with much praise of his virtues; he is proper, wise, witty, and valiant "As Hector" (II.iii.180–87). They alleviate his fears about Beatrice's aggressiveness by a lengthy, exaggerated tale of her desperate passion for him: "Then down upon her knees she falls, weeps, sobs, bears her heart, tears her hair, prays, curses—'O sweet Benedick! God give me patience!'" (II.iii.148–50). The story dovetails perfectly with his fantasy that all women dote on him (and presumably it gratifies the other men to picture the disdainful Beatrice in this helpless state). The men also reassure Benedick that Beatrice is sweet and "out of all suspicion, she is virtuous" (160–61). The gulling permits Benedick to love with his friends' approval while remaining complacently self-satisfied. Even these protective assurances of his power win from him only a grudgingly impersonal acknowledgment of his feelings: "Love me? Why, it must be requited" (II.iii.219). This he must justify by relying, like Claudio, on friends' confirmations of the lady's virtue and marriageability, and by viewing marriage not personally but conventionally as a social institution designed to control desire and ensure procreation: "the world must be peopled" (236).

The women's gulling of Beatrice is utterly different in strategy and effect. They make only one unembroidered mention of Benedick's love for her, and even that is interrogative—"But are you sure / That Benedick loves Beatrice so entirely?" (III.i.36–37). They praise *his* virtues, not Beatrice's. Instead of treating sex with detachment, as the men do with their joke about "'Benedick' and 'Beatrice' between the sheet" (II.iii.139), the women include an explicit, enthusiastic reference to it: "Doth not the gentleman / Deserve as full as fortune a bed / As ever Beatrice shall couch upon?" (III.i.44–46). Throughout most of the staged scene, they attack at length and with gusto Beatrice's proud wit, deflating rather than bolstering her self-esteem. The men emphasize Beatrice's love whereas the women emphasize her inability to love as a means of exorcising it: "She cannot love, / Nor take no shape nor projection of affection, / She is so self-endeared" (54–56). Beatrice, accepting unabashedly the accuracy of these charges— "Contempt, farewell! And maiden pride, adieu!" (109)—is released into an undefensive and personal declaration of love and of passionate submission to Benedick: "Benedick, love on; I will requite thee, / Taming my wild heart to thy loving hand. / If thou dost love, my kindness shall incite thee / To bind our loves up in a holy band" (111–14). She views marriage not as a social inevitability but as a ritual expressing affectionate commitment. Benedick's "love" will be requited with "kindness," not merely with the production of "kind." And, unlike Benedick, she trusts her own sense of his worth more than her friends' praise: "For others say thou dost deserve, and I / Believe it better than reportingly" (115–16). . . .

Male Sexual Anxiety

The anxieties about sexuality and submission that are the source of the men's lovesickness then erupt violently in Don John's slander. It is ironically appropriate that, though Hero has never talked to Claudio at all and he had "never tempted

A book illustration depicting Hero and Claudio in the garden, from Shakespeare's play Much Ado About Nothing. © Blue Lantern Studio/Corbis.

her with word too large" (IV.i.52), he should immediately accept Don John's report that she "talk[ed] with a man out at a window" (IV.i.308) as proof of her infidelity. Though he does not "see her chamber window ent'red" (III.ii.108), this imag-

ined act transforms defensive idealization to vicious degradation. . . . His former cautious, silent worship inverted, Claudio
denounces Hero at their wedding with extravagantly lascivi-
ous, but still conventional, rhetoric:

> Out on thee, seeming! I will write against it.
>
> You seem to me as Dian in her orb,
>
> As chaste as is the bud ere it be blown;
>
> But you are more intemperate in your blood
>
> Than Venus, or those pamp'red animals
>
> That rage in savage sensuality.
>
> [IV.i.55–60]

He perverts the ceremony that had seemed to protect him and
seeks from friends confirmation of her corruption, as he had
formerly needed proof of her virtues.

When unanchored idealization turns to degradation here,
nuptials are shattered more violently and irretrievably than in
the other comedies. The possibility of future reconciliation is
kept alive, however, by the Friar's scheme for Hero's mock
death, by Dogberry and crew's knowledge of the truth about
Don John's deceit, and by Beatrice's command to Benedick.
The slander of Hero tempers Beatrice's commitment to love.
But Claudio's failure of romantic faith in Hero parallels and
helps to rectify Benedick's lack of romantic commitment to
Beatrice. Both men, along with Hero, must risk a comic death
and effect a comic transformation to affirm their love. . . .

The Rehabilitation of Romance

But in *Much Ado* the festive conclusion is not only made possible by Hero's mock death, Claudio's enforced penance, and
Dogberry's apprehension of the "benefactors" who expose the
deceit. Equally important is Benedick's willingness to comply
with Beatrice's command to "Kill Claudio" (IV.i.288). Benedick's acquiescence signals his transformation and reconciles

him with Beatrice. Although the gullings bring Beatrice and Benedick to acknowledge their affections to themselves, they have not risked doing so to each other. The broken nuptials provide the impetus for this commitment. The seriousness of the occasion tempers their wit and strips away their defenses. Weeping for Hero, Beatrice expresses indirectly her vulnerability to Benedick, just as Benedick's assertion of trust in Hero expresses indirectly his love for Beatrice and leads to his direct, ungrudging expression of it: "I do love nothing in the world so well as you" (IV.i.267). This reciprocates Beatrice's earlier vow to "tame her wild heart" for him. But the broken nuptials have encouraged Beatrice to be wary still; her vow is witty, and she asks for more than vows from Benedick, taking seriously his romantic promise, "Come, bid me do anything for thee." "Kill Claudio," she replies (IV.i.287–88).

Extravagant and coercive as her demand may be, Benedick's willingness to comply is a necessary antidote to the play's pervasive misogyny and a necessary rehabilitation of romance from Claudio's corruption of it.[5] Benedick's challenge to Claudio, by affirming his faith in both Hero's and Beatrice's fidelity, repudiates his former mistrust of women and breaks his bonds with the male friends who shared this attitude. Because romantic vows and postures have proved empty or unreliable—"But manhood is melted into cursies, valor into compliment, and men are only turned into tongue, and trim ones too" (IV.i.317–20)—they must now be validated through deeds. The deed Beatrice calls for is of a special sort. Male aggression is to be used not in war but for love, not against women but on their behalf. Beatrice calls on Benedick to become a hero of romance in order to qualify his wit and verify his commitment to her. . . .

The Festive Conclusion

In *Much Ado*, however, Beatrice and Benedick, displacing the Claudio/Hero plot one final time, create the festive conclusion. Disruptive elements continue to be expressed and exorcised in their bantering movement into marriage. Their refusal to love "more than reason" or other than "for pity" or "in friendly recompense" (V.iv.74–93) acknowledges wittily the fear each still has of submission and the desire each has that the other be subordinate. They are finally brought to their nuptials only by a wonderfully comic "miracle," (91) but one not dependent on removal of disguise, recognition of other kinds, or the descent of a god. The discovery of their "halting" sonnets signals their mutual release into the extravagance of romance and is followed by the kiss which, manifesting their mutual desire, serves as a truce in their merry wars. This kiss "stop[s]" Beatrice's mouth as she had earlier urged Hero to "stop" Claudio's at their engagement (V.iv.97; II.i.299). But while affirming mutuality in one way, the kiss ends it in another, for it silences Beatrice for the rest of the play. Similarly, other strong, articulate women are subdued at the ends of their comedies—Julia, Kate, Titania, Rosalind, Viola.[6] This kiss, then, may be seen as marking the beginning of the inequality that Beatrice feared in marriage and that is also implicit in the framing of the wedding festivities with male jokes about cuckoldry, in the reestablishment of male authority by means of these jokes, and in Benedick's control of the nuptials. . . .

Beatrice's and Benedick's sparring is transformed by the broken nuptials into romantic attachment, and Hero's mock death and the revelation of her innocence transform Claudio's degradation of her into a ritualistic penance. Throughout the comedies, broken nuptials, even when initiated by men, give women the power to resist, control, or alter the movement of courtship. But with the celebration of completed nuptials at the end of the comedies, male control is reestablished, and women take their subordinate places in the dance.

Notes

1. *Much Ado*, first published in 1600 and probably written in 1598 or 1599 is around the seventh of the thirteen comedies stretching from *Comedy of Errors* (early 1590)

to *Measure for Measure* (1604). In the introduction to his collection, *Twentieth-Century Interpretations of Much Ado About Nothing* (Englewood Cliffs, N.J.: Prentice-Hall, 1969), Walter R. Davis speaks of the play's "unique transitional status": ". . . largely because of its treatment of evil in society, it forms a bridge between the two halves of Shakespeare's career as comedian" (p. 2).

2. Most critics reluctantly accept the Claudio/Hero story as the "main plot," although they literally or figuratively put the term in quotation marks and are quick to point out that Beatrice and Benedick overshadow this "plot," however "main" it is. See, for example, Graham Story, "The Success of *Much Ado About Nothing*," in Davis, *Twentieth-Century Interpretations*, p. 14; John Crick, "Messina," in ibid., p. 33; and Elliott Krieger, "Social Relations and the Social Order in 'Much Ado About Nothing,'" *Shakespeare Survey* 32 (1979): 50, n. 3. James Smith, "*Much Ado About Nothing*: Notes from a Book in Preparation," *Scrutiny* 13 (1945–46): 242–57, whose claims seem to be somewhat misrepresented in Krieger's footnote, is one of the few critics who argues, as I will, that the two plots depend on each other and to explore psychological and dramatic interdependence as well as thematic relationships among the different parts of the play: Beatrice/Benedick, Claudio/Hero, Dogberry and the Watch, and Don John.

3. Ibid., p. 74, and Barbara Everett, "*Much Ado About Nothing*," *The Critical Quarterly* 3 (1961): 322, both note the positive effects of the displacement of the Hero/Claudio story by the Beatrice/Benedick story. James Smith, in contrast, argues for the impact of Hero's broken nuptials on Beatrice and Benedick: "the tragic scenes of the repudiation of Hero and its immediate consequences would seem to be the centre of the unity in *Much Ado*. Other sections of the play look to them

for completion; themselves, they draw strength and significance from the other sections" (p. 253). Alexander Leggatt, in *Shakespeare's Comedies of Love* (London: Methuen, 1974), pp. 151–83, explores the interplay between naturalism and convention in the play and analyzes how the two plots and the two couples follow parallel movements into convention, with Claudio's and Hero's engendering that of Beatrice and Benedick. Another perspective on the interaction of the two plots is that of John Traugott, who, in "Creating a Rational Rinaldo: A Study in the Mixture of the Genres of Comedy and Romance in *Much Ado About Nothing*," *Genre* 15, nos. 3½ (1982): 157–81, discusses the displacement of romance into comedy which enables the genres to transform each other: "it is this very double-mindedness of romance that invites its 'contamination' by comedy. Its grace will render comedy a new sort of triumph over a scurvy world, its violence and absurdities will have to endure laughter" (p. 158).

4. Editions commonly gloss "bachelors" in this speech as "male or female unmarried persons," claiming that the source of this meaning is the biblical passage, "For when they shall rise from the dead, they neither marry, nor are given in marriage; but are as angels which are in heaven" (Mark 12:25). But the *OED* cites this meaning (5) as rare and obsolete and gives only one reference (Ben Jonson: 1632). In all nineteen other Shakespearean uses, *bachelor* refers exclusively to unmarried men, as it must, for example, in "Such separation as may well be said, / Becomes a virtuous bachelor and maid" (*MND*, (II.i.59–60). When Beatrice claims that "Adam's sons are my brethren" (II.i.60), hopes to join the bachelors in heaven, and wishes she were a man to "eat Claudio's heart out in the market place," she is testifying to the

attractiveness of the world of male comaraderie, a world she would be excluded from after marriage.

5. Traugott, "Creating a Rational Rinaldo" (see n. 3 above), analyzes in somewhat similar fashion the effect of the demand to kill Claudio: "Suddenly our expectations are derailed and they [Beatrice and Benedick] have stolen away the convention of service to the distressed lady, together with its man on horseback, its idealism, its grace, and incongruously incorporated it into the comic charades they concoct between themselves. The wit plot has absorbed the romance plot" (p. 164).

6. Clara Claiborne Park, "As We Like It: How a Girl Can Be Smart and Still Popular," in Lenz et al., *The Woman's Part*, pp. 100–16, discusses how the assertiveness of the heroines is curtailed.

Much Ado About Nothing

Michael Mangan

British scholar Michael Mangan is professor of drama at Lough-borough University in England. A theater director and play-wright as well as a teacher, Mangan is also author of Staging Masculinities: History, Gender, Performance *(2003).*

In the following viewpoint, Michael Mangan contends that the two pairs of lovers in Much Ado About Nothing *depict two completely different approaches to courtship and romantic desire. Claudio and Hero are naive innocents who believe in the shallow conventional attitudes and language of courtship. This approach is consistently satirized in the play. Beatrice and Benedick, on the other hand, represent a more skeptical, even cynical, approach to love and marriage. By the play's end, the bantering and wit combat of these two lovers has turned into a practical, more authentic language of desire.*

Comedies end happily and the happy ending is symbolized by marriage: that, at least, is the conventional view. In *Much Ado About Nothing* there are two sets of couples with, initially, contrasting attitudes towards the comedic happy ending of marriage. Hero and Claudio are the conventional lovers of comedy, for whom the expected wedding day will (supposedly) symbolize the culmination of their desires. This is why the disruption of the ceremony which takes place in act IV, scene i makes for such a painful moment, not only for Hero but for the audience: The promised ending of the narrative has been snatched away, the comedy has collapsed, and the play teeters on the brink of tragedy. And what makes it so poignant is that Hero and Claudio (but especially Hero) had believed in the message which the structure of romantic comedy implies: that the marriage ceremony offers the perfect ending to the story.

Beatrice and Benedick, on the other hand, reject the assumption that marriage makes for a happy ending. Beatrice sees it as a stage in a process of deterioration, and warns Hero that:

> wooing, wedding and repenting is as a Scotch jig, a measure and a cinquepace. The first suit is hot and hasty, like a Scotch jig—and full as fantastical; the wedding mannerly modest, as a measure, full of state and ancientry. And then comes repentance, and with his bad legs falls into the cinquepace faster and faster till he sink into his grave.
> *(II, i, ll. 65–72)*

They are a comic hero and heroine who, at first at least, reject the logic of comedy: the assumption that marriage will see them live happily ever after.

In other plays by Shakespeare those who turn their backs on the forces of Eros (like the lords of Navarre in *Love's Labour's Lost* or Kate in *The Taming of the Shrew*) are usually treated as proud figures heading for a fall. This is how Beatrice and Benedick's friends see them, and in the early scenes the audience is invited to share this point of view—hence the humour of the parallel tricks which are played upon them: It derives from a comfortable shared awareness that Beatrice and Benedick ought to be brought into the comedic marriage arrangements.

I have talked about the trick which their friends play upon them as being benevolent—designed to do them good. There is another way of looking at it, however, which does not contradict that but which stresses another aspect of the trick. As we saw in the early chapters of this book, laughter can be used as a weapon against those who flout the norms of a society; it can be used to discourage socially deviant behaviour. Beatrice and Benedick's 'deviancy' lies in their professed rejection of the pattern of comedy. The trick which is played upon them is a way of mobilizing the laughter of the audience in order to bring them back into line, and to make them behave according to the expected norms—not so much of their society as of their genre.

As the play progresses, however, the conventional model of romantic love, represented by Hero and Claudio, becomes increasingly compromised. Seen from Claudio's point of view it is compromised by Hero's supposed faithlessness; more importantly, seen from the point of view of the audience (who knows the truth of the matter) it is compromised by the ease with which Claudio's adoration collapses into loathing. The audience is made more and more uncomfortably aware that Beatrice and Benedick may be justified in their original suspicions of love and marriage as they exist in Messina. And the more the relationship between Beatrice and Benedick develops, the more the one between Hero and Claudio is brought into question.

Throughout the play, the courtship of Hero and Claudio is compared and contrasted in this way with that of Beatrice and Benedick. In many respects the two courtships are each other's opposite: In one respect, though, they are similar, in that both courtships are initially frustrated by the couples' inability to express love directly. The disguised Don Pedro has to speak for Claudio, taking his place in the courtship ritual and speaking the words that Claudio himself seems unable to say. It is only when his path has thus been cleared for him that he can assume in full his role of the lover, and speak the poetic language of love. The moment is pointed up by Beatrice:

> LEONATO: Count, take of me my daughter, and
> with her my fortunes. His Grace hath made
> the match, and all grace say amen to it!
>
> BEATRICE: Speak, Count, it is your cue.
>
> CLAUDIO: Silence is the perfectest herald of
> joy. I were but little happy if I could say

how much. Lady, as you are mine, I am
yours. I give myself away for you and dote
upon the exchange.

(II, i, ll. 199–306)

Claudio's 'silence' is eloquently expressed: When he finally
manages to speak, he does so in 'festival terms', speaking a formal and poetic language of love. Benedick calls it 'orthogra-
phy . . . a very fantastical banquet' and laments for the old
days when Claudio 'was wont to speak plain and to the purpose, like an honest man and a soldier' (II, iii, ll. 20–1). In fact
Claudio tends to compartmentalize his languages: He has one
register for laughing and joking with the boys, and another
very different one for going courting. This compartmentaliz-
ing of languages corresponds, in fact, to the way in which he
compartmentalizes his emotional life. It is on a par with his
idealization and subsequent demonization of Hero, and with
his ability to dissociate himself from his own cruelty in reject-
ing her.

In the early part of the play the pattern of courtship which
Claudio and Hero follow is gently satirized. It appears to be
presented as a not-too-exaggerated caricature of a kind of
courtship which is familiar in Elizabethan drama. It is based
at least in part on economic considerations: Claudio's first
question to Don Pedro concerns Leonato and whether he has
a son; Don Pedro reassures Claudio that Hero is 'his only heir'
(I, i, ll. 278). The pair do not know each other intimately, and
the love that they feel for each other is one based on a sense
of affinity which is formed at a distance. It is a love which has
not yet developed a sexual dimension beyond that of erotic
attraction: Claudio insists that he

. . . never tempted her with word too large,

But as a brother to his sister showed

Bashful sincerity and comely love.

(IV, i, ll. 52–4)

Even the intimacy of a person-to-person declaration of love is not initially available to them and the betrothal itself is as much a matter between Don Pedro and Leonato as it is between Hero and Claudio. Moreover, the fact that things should be done this way does not seem to cause anyone any particular surprise. Don Pedro takes on the surrogate courtship almost as a matter of course.

> DON PEDRO: . . . If thou dost love fair Hero, cherish it,
>
> And I will break with her, and with her father,
>
> And thou shalt have her. Was't not to this end
>
> That though began'st to twist so fine a story?
>
> CLAUDIO: How sweetly you do minister to love,
>
> That know love's grief by his complexion!
>
> But lest my liking might too sudden seem
>
> I would have salved it with a longer treatise.
>
> DON PEDRO: What need the bridge much broader than the flood?
>
> The fairest grant is the necessity.
>
> Look what will serve is fit. 'Tis once: thou lovest
>
> And I will fit thee with the remedy.
>
> (I, i, ll. 291–302)

And yet within these parameters Claudio's dramatic function as the 'young lover' remains intact: The audience is to understand that he is 'in love' with Hero. 'The sweetest lady that ever I looked on' (I, i, l. 181), he calls her, and we are meant to believe him. The level-headed Elizabethan considerations of family formation are overlaid with a passionate language of courtly love, and for a while it looks as if it will be an anti-dote to the cynicism of Beatrice and Benedick and the buckish jesting of the male comrades-in-arms.

But in the second part of the play the gentle mockery turns into savage irony, as Claudio's courtly love and his lyri-cal, distant idealizing of a woman whom he has wooed at second-hand turns out to have a sinister reverse side to it. In the scene which by rights should have marked the culmina-tion of the love plot, the stately, courtly language of the be-trothal is replaced by the verbal violence of Claudio's public humiliation and rejection of Hero.

CLAUDIO: . . . Father, by your leave,

Will you with free and unconstrained soul

Give me this maid your daughter?

LEONATO: As freely, son, as God did give her me.

CLAUDIO: And what have I to give you back whose worth

May counterpoise this rich and precious gift?

DON PEDRO: Nothing, unless you render her again.

CLAUDIO: Sweet Prince, you learn me noble thankfulness.

There, Leonato, take her back again.

Give not this rotten orange to your friend.

(IV, i, ll. 22–31)

The audience knows, more or less, what is about to happen. We are aware (as Leonato is not) that the polite civilities of the Prince and his *protégé* are bogus, and that the exchange between Claudio and Don Pedro contains a double meaning quite the opposite of what Leonato expects. Even so, the image of the 'rotten orange' which Claudio uses to describe the woman everybody thinks he is about to marry, is a shockingly violent one, and one which shatters the atmosphere of celebration. The marriage ceremony turns into a punitive shaming ritual, in which Hero is publicly humiliated as surely as if she were in the pillory or ducking-stool.

Even more violent than Claudio's insult is Leonato's almost hysterical reaction to the charge. Siding immediately with Claudio, his public rejection of his daughter takes on the intensity of a curse:

Grieved I, I had but one?

Chid I for that at frugal nature's frame?

O one too much by thee! Why had I one?

Why ever wast thou lovely in my eyes?

Why had I not with charitable hand

Took up a beggar's issue at my gates,

Who smirched thus and mired with infamy,

I might have said, 'No part of it is mine;

This shame derives itself from unknown loins'?

But mine, and mine I loved, and mine I praised,

And mine that I was proud on, mine so much

That I myself was to myself not mine,

Valuing of her—why she, O, she is fall'n

Into a pit of ink. . .

(IV, i, ll. 126–39)

The fact that the daughter is the property of the father is stressed in this speech; the word 'mine' pounds through Leonato's lines with a drumbeat insistence. His disgust at his daughter's supposed infidelity and his desire to disown her only serve to intensify his sense that she is, indeed, his to dispose of as he pleases.

Lewis Carroll asked why Hero does not provide herself with an alibi. Yet it is significant how little notice is taken of what Hero herself says in this scene. Elsewhere in the play Hero is presented as a lively and interesting young woman, particularly when she is 'in private', in the company of her female friends. When Claudio is on stage, however, she becomes demure and quiet. In the scene in which she was betrothed to Claudio she was given almost nothing to say. Now, as she is rejected by him, most of her talking is once more done for her by the dominant males in her life: her future husband, her father, or her Prince. She is not, however, completely silent. In answer to Claudio's accusations she protests her innocence:

Is my lord well, that he should speak so
wide?. . .

O God defend me! How am I beset!

What kind of catechizing call you this?. . .

Is [my name] not Hero? Who can blot that
name

With any just reproach?. . .

I talked with no man at that hour, my lord.

(IV, i, ll. 62, 76–77, 81–2, 85)

Yet her words are ignored. Claudio does not believe her; Leonato apparently does not even hear her! 'She not denies it'

(IV, i, ll. 175), he exclaims, quite erroneously, and he deduces from her non-denial a proof of her guilt. The language of the public scene belongs entirely to men; the woman's words are not listened to.

Thus the conventional love relationship, as exemplified by Hero and Claudio, becomes less and less attractive as the play develops. We see the interesting young woman diminished by her relationship with the man. Even in fortune Hero's role in the relationship is a passive one. Things are done *to* her: Her marriage is arranged with her having scarcely a line to say about it, and later she is treated like a piece of faulty merchandise both by her father and her future husband as they find their projected idealization of her under threat. Her passive role turns into that of victim.

Claudio, meanwhile, appears increasingly repulsive: As a wooer he was unimpressive, but as a potential life partner he is appalling. He exemplifies perfectly a kind of masculine attitude to women which can cope with them only as extremes: Thus, deprived of his idealized image of Hero as pure virgin, he reacts by castigating her as a whore.

> CLAUDIO: Out on thee, seeming! I will write against it.
>
> You seem to me as Dian in her orb,
>
> As chaste as is the bud ere it be blown.
>
> But you are more intemperate in your blood
>
> Than Venus or those pampered animals
>
> That rage in savage sensuality.
>
> (IV, i, ll. 56–60)

By this stage in the play the bantering, jokey language of the inhabitants of Messina is being shown in a very different light. In earlier scenes it had been presented as something quite attractive: good humour, camaraderie, high spirits. As the play progresses, however, the jokes and the wordplay are seen more and more clearly as a mode of discourse which serves to limit the characters' emotional range. The most striking example of this is given in act V, scene i, where Don Pedro and Claudio, refusing to accept any responsibility for Hero's supposed death, try to revert to their earlier modes of speech. Having shrugged off Leonato's challenge, they turn with relief to Benedick, trying almost desperately to get him to join in with their jesting in an attempt to prove to themselves that nothing has really changed.

> CLAUDIO: We have been up and down to seek thee; for we are high proof melancholy, and would fain have it beaten away. Wilt thou use thy wit?
>
> BENEDICK: It is in my scabbard. Shall I draw it?
>
> DON PEDRO: Dost thou wear thy wit by thy side?
>
> CLAUDIO: Never any did so, though very many have been beside their wit. I will bid thee draw, as we do the minstrels: draw to pleasure us.
>
> DON PEDRO: As I am an honest man, he looks pale. Art thou sick, or angry?
>
> CLAUDIO: What, courage, man! What though care killed a cat, thou hast mettle enough in thee to kill care.
>
> (V, i, ll. 122–33)

The jokes here sound increasingly hollow and forced, not because they are intrinsically any less witty than the earlier banter of the men, but because the context has turned them sour. They need Benedick to join in with their game in order to reassure themselves that things are as they always were: the language of wit is here being used by both men as a shelter behind which to hide. Claudio's resolute lack of response to the news of Hero's 'death' has already made us realize that he will hear only what he wants to hear. Now, as Benedick, charged with the duty to 'kill Claudio', attempts to challenge him to a duel, Claudio and Don Pedro try not to hear the seriousness in his tone. When Benedick not only refuses to humour them, but finally does make his challenge heard, Don Pedro (ironically) puts it down to the corrupting influence of love! But the Prince's exclamation that 'He is in earnest' (V, i, ll. 193) indicates his shocked realization that the camaraderie is at an end; Benedick has dropped his role of jester, and by ceasing to joke he has broken the fellowship.

And yet the language of jokes is reinstated at the very end of the play. Just as Leonato's trick about the 'second Hero' reclaims the practical joke as a benign device, so the jokes which seemed to turn sour in act V, scene i become lighthearted and celebratory again in the final scene. Whereas most of the characters seem to feel that they must choose either to make jokes or to be in love, Beatrice and Benedick end up by having their cake and eating it. As Benedick says, he and Beatrice are 'too wise to woo peaceably' (V, ii, l. 65); they find, though, that they are able to court each other with banter and jokes—in the very terms, in fact, in which they once abused each other. They reject the language of romantic love in favour of a more everyday language. Benedick, it is true, makes a halfhearted stab at love poetry, but soon gives up:

BENEDICK: . . . Marry, I cannot show it in
rhyme. I have tried. I can find out no rhyme
to 'lady' but 'baby', an innocent rhyme; for
'scorn' 'horn', a hard rhyme; for 'school'
'fool', a babbling rhyme. Very ominous end-
ings. No, I was not born under a rhyming
planet. I cannot woo in festival terms.

(V, ii, ll. 34–9)

For Beatrice and Benedick, their jokes become a means to resist the kind of love match exemplified by Hero and Claudio. By the end of the play they have constructed a loving relationship which is as much of a sparring match as their enmity was.

> BENEDICK: Come, I will have thee; but by this
> light I take thee for pity.

> BEATRICE: I would not deny you; but by this
> good day I yield upon great persuasion, and
> partly to save your life, for I was told you
> were in a consumption.

(V, iv, ll. 92–6)

The 'happy end' which sees Hero married off to Claudio is fraught with contradictions, for the conventional relationship founded on romantic love which they exemplify has been severely satirized by Shakespeare. Beatrice and Benedick are offered as an alternative to Hero and Claudio. The festive ending is displaced onto the couple who have managed to deploy their jokes and their bantering not only as a defence against desire, but also as a language of desire. Their relationship—for all its anomalies—is a more equal one than either of them might have expected. In their Messina, unlike in the Padua of *The Taming of the Shrew*, there is no longer any need for the husband to 'win', for him to browbeat the wife into submission as Petruchio does. Beatrice and Benedick end the play more or less even on points, with the promise of frequent friendly rematches in the future. And if the relationship between the pair is not presented as an ideal, it is nonetheless seen as preferable to the fragility of an idealized romantic love such as Claudio's with all its tendency to collapse into loathing and disgust. And for Beatrice and Benedick to have wrested the language—and the laughter—to their own ends in this way is in itself some cause for celebration.

Cross-Dressing and Courtship in *As You Like It*

Penny Gay

Penny Gay is a professor of English and drama at the University of Sydney in Australia. Among her various scholarly writings, she has edited Shakespeare's As You Like It *(1998) and authored* As She Likes It: Shakespeare's Unruly Women *(1994).*

Satire of pastoral conventions about courtship is clearly central to As You Like It, *according to scholar Penny Gay. However, another energy seems to overtake the play, as Shakespeare delights in bending conventional gender roles through his disguised heroine Rosalind. Gay explains that when Rosalind cross-dresses as a man, she is liberated from conventional female gender rules, and she gains self-knowledge through the power of language and wit. In her banishment and her disguise, the charismatic Rosalind finds freedom to express love and desire in wholly new ways.*

Unlike the realistic community of *Much Ado* [*About Nothing*]'s Messina, *As You Like It* is structured around a symbolic contrast familiar to Elizabethan audiences: the court and the country. This contrast was the mainstay of one of the most popular of Elizabethan literary genres, the pastoral. It was to be found in sonnets and songs (including many madrigals), in verse dialogues or eclogues, including an influential work by the major nondramatic poet of the period, Edmund Spenser (*The Shepheardes Calender*, 1579), and in novels such as Thomas Lodge's *Rosalynde* (1590) on which Shakespeare based his play. It contrasted the lives of idealised shepherds and shepherdesses with the behaviour of the educated men and women of the court. Each of these claimed to envy the life of the other—natural simplicity or courtly sophistication.

Writing the play in 1599, Shakespeare took advantage of his audience's familiarity with this fashion. But he took it into areas that they could not have predicted, largely by layering it with his own interests in the politics of gender, a field that he had begun exploring in the comedies written up to this point. *As You Like It* is more famous, now, for the charismatic role of the cross-dressed Rosalind than for its satire of pastoral conventions. . . . By having Rosalind self-consciously and pleasurably play the girl playing the boy playing the girl—and originally, it was of course a boy actor playing the girl Rosalind—Shakespeare stages the *fluidity* of gender construction for our instruction and delight.

Just as Beatrice is on the periphery of Leonato's household [in *Much Ado About Nothing*], and—importantly—fatherless, so is Rosalind, the heroine of *As You Like It*, cousin and best friend of the more conventional young woman, Celia. Once again, this marginal position enables behaviour that would not be possible for the conventional girl. But then there's a surprising development. At the end of act 1, when Rosalind has been banished simply for being her exiled father's daughter, Celia declares that she will not play the obedient daughter, but will run away with Rosalind, 'To liberty, and not to banishment.' Thus, even though much of the rest of the play concerns the cross-dressed Rosalind's doubly disguised wooing of Orlando, there is also a deployment of the theme of sisterhood—the strong and mutually supportive bonds, going back to childhood, between two very different adult women. Throughout the play Celia (also, let us remember, a cross-dressed boy actor originally) functions in this sisterly role as well as in the role of conventional feminine and genteel young woman who attempts to rein in the excesses of Rosalind's cross-dressed indecorum.

Banishment and Disguise

The play begins with a quarrel between two brothers—Oliver, the elder brother who has claimed all their father's estate, and Orlando, the dispossessed youngest son. It begins, that is, with the typical masculine concerns of the folktale narrative— 'There comes an old man and his three sons', as Le Beau puts it (1.2.93). The whole of act 1 is set in this world of male power and the violence associated with it: Orlando's attack on his brother, out of frustrated rage, a mere forty lines into the play; his bout with the famously violent Charles the wrestler in 1.2 (when he unexpectedly wins this, there is the first glimmer of reassurance for the audience that the traditional folktale success of the youngest son will indeed come about); finally, the tyrannical banishment of Rosalind by Duke Frederick.

When Rosalind and Celia decide to leave this oppressive male-dominated environment and flee to the Forest of Arden, they make significant decisions about their costumes, and thus their public identities. Rosalind opts for the appearance of masculinity, a swashbuckling hunter with echoes of commedia's Capitano (with *two* phallic weapons):

ROSALIND: Were it not better,

Because that I am more than common tall,

That I did suit me all points like a man,

A gallant curtal-axe upon my thigh,

A boar-spear in my hand, and in my heart

Lie there what hidden woman's fear there will,

We'll have a swashing and a martial outside,

As many other mannish cowards have

That do outface it with their semblances.

(1.3.104–12)

Celia decides to put herself 'in poor and mean attire, / And with a kind of umber smirch [her] face'—that is, to take a major drop in class status, though retaining the appearance of a woman (and thus also the vulnerability of her gender, unlike Rosalind). These decisions involve renamings; the young women will no longer bear the names that their godparents gave them at their church christening, but make their own decisions about who they are:

CELIA: What shall I call thee when thou art a man?

ROSALIND: I'll have no worse a name than Jove's own page,

And therefore look you call me 'Ganymede'.

But what will you be called?

CELIA: Something that hath a reference to my state:

No longer 'Celia' but 'Aliena'.

(1.3.113–18)

Both names are easily decodable by the audience. Ganymede is the young male lover of the pagan god Jove, and slang for homosexual toy-boy in Elizabethan English. Aliena (a made-up name) refers to Celia's newly outcast state. Celia's excited couplet at the end of act 1—'Now go we in content, / To liberty, and not to banishment'—has striking connotations: Like their renaming of themselves, the word 'banishment' can be reinterpreted as that most dangerous of political cries, 'Liberty!'. . .

Rosalind's Cross-Dressing

Rosalind not only changes in appearance, from court lady to hunter to shepherd boy, she also changes her behaviour, from being the less talkative and slightly more subdued of the two girls in act 1 (Celia, after all, is in her own home, Rosalind is a

Actors Elisabeth Bergner and Sophie Stewart play Rosalind and Celia, respectively, in direc-tor Paul Czinner's 1936 film of Shakespeare's As You Like It. © Moviepix/Getty Images.

guest and the daughter of the exiled Duke), to playing the elo-quently witty and outrageously flirtatious Ganymede for the remaining four acts of the play. We might well infer that her 'true self' has been released by the change of costume, gender, and situation. Or we might simply say that she is seizing an opportunity, in the temporary space of liberty that is the For-est of Arden, to talk and talk, and take the lead in a courtship situation. For the first time in her life, she is unconstrained by conventional notions of femininity. Arguably, the original theatre audience was observing, perhaps for the first time, the spectacle of a woman dominating the conversation but divorced from the notion that this is 'shrewish' behaviour.

Rosalind talks mainly in prose, not blank verse (so, largely, does Beatrice). Prose allows for fluid, complex, unpredictable verbal play, because it's not constrained by the traditions of rhetoric that accompany blank verse. In fact, Rosalind's only substantial blank verse speech is in 3.5, to Phebe, where she needs to play the authoritative male—and seems to revel in it:

And why, I pray you? Who might be your
mother

That you insult, exult, and all at once

Over the wretched? What, though you have
no beauty,

As, by my faith, I see no more in you

Than without candle may go dark to bed,

Must you be therefore proud and pitiless?

. . . 'Tis not your inky brows, your black silk
hair,

Your bugle eyeballs, nor your cheek of
cream

That can entame my spirits to your worship.

. . . But, mistress, know yourself. Down on
your knees,

And thank heaven, fasting, for a good man's
love;

For I must tell you friendly in your ear,

Sell when you can: you are not for all mar-
kets.

(3.6.34–60)

Amusingly, even this schoolmasterly bluntness has no power
over the besotted Phebe, rapt as she is in the conventions of
courtly love: 'Sweet youth, I pray you chide a year together; / I
had rather hear you chide than this man woo', she replies
(3.6.64–5).

Rosalind's wooing scenes with Orlando are the most remarkable of her performances as the androgynous Ganymede.
They operate through a freewheeling, witty, erudite satirisa-
tion and deconstruction of Petrarchanism. The conventions of
courtly love drive romantic relationships in popular literature;
they are reliably productive of sighs, weeping, irrationality, ob-
session—everything that we see young Silvius suffering for the
unrequited love of Phebe; and everything that, thankfully, Orlando is not. He does *not* have a lean cheek, neglected beard,
ungartered hose, untied shoes (3.2). Orlando, that is, whatever
his failings as a poet—we have heard his excruciating verses to
Rosalind ('tedious homilies', she says)—is a healthy young
man driven by desire to do *something* to sublimate his passion. Thus, he is a ready collaborator with Rosalind's plan to
pretend to be his lady love and thereby 'cure' him of his passion. Although he claims, 'I would not be cured, youth', by the
end of this scene he has given in to Rosalind's charismatic insistence on offering him some substitute for his absent beloved. To see how this has come about we need to go back
earlier into the scene, before Orlando even arrives.

In the long opening discussion between Rosalind and Celia we see and hear a Rosalind who is herself just as hyperac-
tively in love as Orlando is. She doesn't have the courtly lover's
option of writing poems and 'abusing' trees; all she can do is
talk to—or at—her best friend. The energy of her speech, its
piled-up unanswered questions, its outlandish metaphors, ex-
plodes like a fireworks show:

ROSALIND: Good my complexion, dost thou
think, though I am caparisoned [dressed]
like a man, I have a doublet and hose in my
disposition? One inch of delay more is a
South Sea of discovery. I prithee tell me
who is it—quickly, and speak apace. I would
thou couldst stammer that thou might'st
pour this concealed man out of thy mouth
as wine comes out of a narrow-mouthed
bottle: either too much at once or none at
all. I prithee take the cork out of thy mouth
that I may drink thy tidings.

(3.3.162–9)

Celia can barely get a word in, but finally assures Rosalind of
what she wanted to hear, and receives another manic response:

ROSALIND: Alas the day, what shall I do with
my doublet and hose? What did he when
thou saw'st him? What said he? How looked
he? Wherein went he? What makes he here?
Did he ask for me? Where remains he? How
parted he with thee, and when shalt thou
see him again? Answer me in one word.

(3.3.181–8)

This energy impels into her hailing Orlando 'like a saucy
lackey', and beginning the first long witty exchange with him.
It seemingly doesn't actually matter what they are talking
about, just that they should display to each other their vitality,
their wit, their suitability to be a couple. (It is no wonder that
Orlando doesn't recognise her—both were virtually speechless
in their meeting in act 1.) They have none of the backstory of
Beatrice and Benedick, so there is no spikiness in their exchange, just delight. For Orlando, someone to talk to, at last!—

and clearly more fun than the solemn rhetoric of the Duke in exile and the melancholy Jaques (his only conversation with Jaques is in lines 214–49 of this scene; they part by mutual agreement).

Verbal Energy and Wit

Their second courtship scene, 4.1—this time introduced by a slightly edgy conversation between Jaques and Rosalind—while still driven by the same verbal energy, is more fraught. Rosalind complains of Orlando's lateness; he offers to kiss her (she evades this alarming move with more words); he complains of continuing frustration and threatens to 'die' like a true Petrarchan. This produces another extraordinary speech from Rosalind, critiquing the whole literary tradition of courtly love for its ignorance of emotional realism:

> No, faith, die by attorney. The poor world is almost six thousand years old and in all this time there was not any man died in his own person, videlicet [namely], in a love-cause. Troilus had his brains dashed out with a Grecian club, yet he did what he could to die before, and he is one of the patterns of love; Leander, he would have lived many a fair year though Hero had turned nun, if it had not been for a hot midsummer night, for, good youth, he went but forth to wash him in the Hellespont and, being taken with the cramp, was drowned, and the foolish chroniclers of that age found it was Hero of Sestos. But these are all lies: men have died from time to time—and worms have eaten them—but not for love.
>
> (4.1.75–85)

Rosalind's verbal display regains her the advantage. She uses it to demand that Celia 'marry' them, and, overcoming Celia's objection that she 'cannot say the words' (Celia is always conscious of the rules of femininity), Rosalind brings about a most audacious theatrical moment. She instructs Celia in the words to be spoken by the priest in the church service—and as if that wasn't sacrilegious enough, she then ensures that both she and Orlando speak the lines that constitute a legal marriage in Elizabethan society:

> ROSALIND: . . . you must say, 'I take thee, Rosalind, for wife.'
>
> ORLANDO: I take thee, Rosalind, for wife.
>
> ROSALIND: I might ask you for your commission; but I do take thee, Orlando, for my husband.
>
> (4.1.108–12)

Excited, perhaps slightly embarrassed banter follows this moment (often the actors do kiss at this point, just as in most weddings); and when Orlando extricates himself claiming an appointment with the Duke, Rosalind again expresses in charged prose to her confidante, the outraged Celia, the depth of her passion: 'O coz, coz, coz, my pretty little coz, that thou didst know how many fathom deep I am in love!' (4.1.165–6).

The Revelation of Truth

Finally, there comes a point when Orlando (now actually wounded in the fight with the lioness, *not* metaphorically 'wounded' by love) says, 'I can live no longer by thinking'—or imagining. Rosalind offers to bring the play's 'idle talking' to an end, and to do so with the assistance of 'magic' that the audience knows to be theatrical: to 'set [Rosalind] before your eyes . . . human as she is'. It is time, that is, for the action that only she can bring about, the revelation of truth. We might say that since she's been liberated into eloquent, daring speech, she has recognised her own power, her 'unfeminine' energy that can be put to good use in a world where—at least temporarily—patriarchal power doesn't entirely rule.

There is a poignant but inevitable irony to this conclusion. Comedy, while delighting in the events of a briefly topsy-turvy world, is ultimately conservative: Its mission is to revitalise the social status quo by reincorporating the energies of the 'outlandish', through the institution of marriage in particular. As soon as she reappears in female costume, and makes the ritual reassignment of herself to her astonished father and husband, Rosalind is silent (like Beatrice) until the play finishes. But Shakespeare has one more trick up his theatrical sleeve. There is the traditional dance, commanded by the now restored Duke Senior. It is followed by Rosalind's extraordinary, unexpected, and indecorous epilogue:

> It is not the fashion to see the lady the Epilogue; but it is no more unhandsome than to see the lord the Prologue . . . My way is to conjure you, and I'll begin with the women. I charge you, O women, for the love you bear to men, to like as much of this play as please you.—And I charge you, O men, for the love you bear to women—as I perceive by your simpering none of you hates them—that between you and the women the play may please. If I were a woman, I would kiss as many of you as had beards that pleased me, complexions that liked me, and breaths that I defied not. And I am sure as many as have good beards, or good faces, or sweet breaths will, for my kind offer, when I make curtsey, bid me farewell.

Although Shakespearean epilogues normally act as a 'bridge' for the audience back to the real world, this one actually takes us back into the world of the play, where gender is fluid and undetermined, dependent only on the choice of the performer. It leaves the audience delightfully confused, sure of only one thing: the charismatic presence of the actor playing Rosalind.

Sexuality and the Law in *Measure for Measure*

Bernice W. Kliman and Laury Magnus

A prolific writer and editor of Shakespeare's plays, Bernice W. Kliman was best known for her pioneering work on film productions of Shakespeare. At the time of her death in 2011, she was professor of English at Nassau Community College. Laury Magnus, professor of English at the United States Merchant Marine Academy, is coeditor of the recent book Who Hears in Shakespeare? *(2012).*

In Measure for Measure, *Shakespeare depicts a wide range of sexual behaviors, including religious celibacy, prostitution, premarital pregnancy, and attempted rape. According to Kliman and Magnus, our response to these issues is shaped primarily by two characters, Duke Vincentio and the novice nun Isabella. Isabella's dilemma—whether to preserve her chastity or save her brother's life—is the central problem of the play. While the Duke intervenes to protect a number of powerless characters in the play, Kliman and Magnus contend that he also appears to manipulate the feelings of others for his own purposes.*

Sex, seduction, betrayal, disguise, death sentences, reprieves, courtroom drama, a corrupt, hypocritical judge, and a ruler-in-disguise observing all this along with audiences— these are the heady elements from which *Measure for Measure* springs. The beauty and power of the play are manifested in some of the most resonant poetry in Shakespeare's canon, whether it voices the poignancy of a condemned man coming to grips with his own mortality, the spiritual torment of a magistrate in the throes of illicit desire, or the futile outrage of a woman facing gross injustice wielded without mercy or conscience. Written just a couple of years after Shakespeare's most mature comedies, such as *Twelfth Night* and *As You Like It, Measure for Measure* is, by comparison, a very dark comedy, and one whose denouement leaves many issues unresolved. The play's plot construction makes audiences think as much as respond emotionally. If, with its rough, crude, bawdy, and low-minded characters like Lucio or Pompey, the play is comedic, it also stages unforgettable scenes of intense conflict.

Laws Controlling Sexuality

Measure for Measure's ambiguity about whether its main characters, the Duke and Isabella, are admirable or despicable is one of the reasons critics have called it a problem play. In performance, these characters can tend toward either extreme, or with subtle gradations in between: some directors want audiences to rejoice with the pair at the end when they find a truer love than any other in the play; other directors relish the opportunity to darken their characters, exposing defects in Vienna as they mirror in many ways our own attitudes towards sex and money.

The Duke's substitute, Angelo, condemns sexuality no matter what form it takes, whether thoughtless and empty coupling, prostitution, or sex as a result of mutual love. Implicitly, the Duke accepts Angelo's view of sexuality. Though he had been lax in applying the laws in Venice, the Duke says that he has chosen Angelo because he can be firmer than the Duke had been. But through his observation of the effects of the strong application of the law, the Duke himself comes to a more reasoned and nuanced view of sexuality.

The Duke protects the powerless, especially women, against the sexual predation common in Vienna. He finds a way to prevent the rape of Isabella by Angelo—ironically, the officer who administers the law against fornication. He also gives

Mariana, formerly engaged to Angelo, a chance for a husband, which Angelo had denied to her doubly by accusing her of "lightness" (the sort of thing that in some societies still gets a woman whipped in the public square) and citing also the loss of her dowry as his justification for breaking the vow he made to her years earlier. Kate Keepdown is also the recipient of the Duke's ameliorating intervention. She is a prostitute who has had a child by Lucio, as Lucio freely admits, but she and her child both are righted at the end by the Duke's forcing Lucio to marry her. (Though she is not physically present in the original script, most modern productions bring her on as a silent character.) Whether these two marriages will be happy or not is beside the point; marriage is the only solution possible, and while an audience may see onstage expressions of Angelo's reluctance to be married to Mariana and Lucio's decided aversion to be married to Kate Keepdown, marriage is a fair if not a happy solution for the women. Having saved Claudio from death, the Duke also can see that Claudio and Juliet have the consummation that they had wished for all along: that is, marriage and legitimacy for their child. All of these situations are sexual, having to do with Viennese society's mistaken ideas about many aspects of love and lust.

Sexuality and Money

Money plays an integral role in the play's sexual subtext; its influence is subtly woven into the play's conflicts. Isabella has chosen to be a novice in the order of Poor Clares, a Franciscan order that pledges poverty. Novitiates in that order were not (and still are not) required to pay a dowry to enter the order, nor were their families expected to support them in any way. In performance, not very much need be made of the reason for Isabella's choice of this particular sect. Probably a modern audience—or even Shakespeare's audience—would not understand the nature of the Poor Clares and the reason for Shakespeare's choice. But an actor and director could show that Isabella's whole heart is not in the choice she has made by the way she speaks her first line in the play: "And have you nuns no farther privileges?" (1.4.1). We discover that Claudio and Juliet have made love before a formal marriage ceremony only because her family would not provide a dowry for them. We also infer that Claudio's and Isabella's parents are dead, and that however religious Isabella may actually be, her decision to enter a nunnery is at least partly motivated by poverty. Neither she nor Claudio has money.

Mariana, to "get herself a better husband," if indeed the Duke were to execute Angelo, would require the money that Angelo's estate would give her. We can guess that women such as Kate Keepdown and Mrs. Overdone follow their profession because they have no other way to earn their keep. Only when Pompey finds employment as an assistant to the executioner at the prison can he give up his trade of pimp.

Shakespeare chose Vienna as his setting for two reasons: first, at that time the Duke was the absolute ruler of his city-state, and secondly, Vienna, which was Catholic, allowed him to feature friars and nuns. A double complication at the play's beginning gives rise to the action of *Measure for Measure*: On the one hand, the Duke mysteriously withdraws from his own kingdom and abdicates his power as ruler in Vienna, and on the other, he returns disguised as a friar to observe, with fresh eyes, his deputies' execution of their duties. As a political experiment, this withdrawal and disguised return seems to have mirrored King James's situation and behavior. James was both a seasoned King of Scotland (like Duke Vincentio) and a new ruler (like Angelo) of an unfamiliar England when he assumed the English throne in 1603. In March of 1604, he also made a disguised excursion into his subjects' lives to meditate on his challenges as a ruler, undertaking a "would-be secret visit to the [London] Exchange to observe merchants' behavior, while he himself remained incognito".

Justice and Religion

But in the play, Duke Vincentio's apparent withdrawal from Vienna is sudden, mysterious, unexplained. All we learn from his terse opening lines is that he is giving Angelo power as his substitute, with Escalus as his second, enjoining them to use the full scope of the law, to show both its "mortality and mercy" (1.1.44). It is not till act 1, scene 3, when he speaks with Friar Thomas, that we learn at least part of the Duke's motivation: Conscious of having been too lax in executing the law and of having allowed sexual license to reign freely, he feels that his deputies will be in a much better position to apply the law strictly for the deterrence of crime and sin. As in other mature comedies and romances such as *The Merchant of Venice* and *The Tempest*, questions abound concerning the relations between the neglect or abuse of the law and the potential restoration of the balance of justice. In many of Shakespeare's plays, such restoration derives from a ruler's finding room in his heart for mercy over severity. But as this play opens, mercy, like oppressive harshness, seems to create its own problems in the unregenerate stews of corrupt Vienna. In the scenes following the Duke's departure, the two deputies who substitute for the Duke appear as anything but true deputies to the absent regent—himself supposed to be God's deputy on earth. We see that the deputies' execution of the law is arbitrary and capricious. Angelo feels himself above dealing with the petty crimes of characters such as Pompey and Froth, though their garbled testimony implies that they *have* committed sexual crimes. Escalus, trying in his own way to mete out justice with patient deliberation, is nevertheless unable or unwilling to come down hard on the likes of Pompey the pimp, or, perhaps more to the point, on the well-connected, wealthy but empty-headed Froth, an incorrigible frequenter of brothels. Escalus has an unfortunate weakness for the well-connected or wealthy. He argues for Claudio on the basis, among other ameliorating factors, that he "had a most noble

117

father" (2.1.7). On the other hand, Angelo's puritanical rigidity in sentencing Claudio to immediate doom for premarital sex is a terrifying "severity," one which both the provost and Escalus criticize behind Angelo's back. They are sadly conscious of their lack of power to influence Angelo. (Thus both characters are dramatic foils to Isabella, who also fails in her more intense attempts to persuade Angelo to show mercy.) Angelo's passion leads him to diabolical excesses no less horrid because they cause *him* horror and self-loathing. More troubling, it is soon revealed that the Duke-as-friar is (or has become) aware of Angelo's past desertion of Mariana and of his hypocrisy in seeming to be so much holier than others: "We shall see if power change purpose," the Duke declares, "what our seemers be" (1.3.54). And yet, in the habit of a friar, the Duke, after learning of Angelo's effort to rape Isabella, continues to rest his confidence in Angelo's essential goodness. He assumes that Angelo's unscrupulous behavior is an aberration and expects him to grant Claudio's pardon once Isabella has tricked him into thinking she has yielded to his lust.

Sexuality and Religious Belief

Understanding the play's religious background can be a challenge for contemporary audiences. In Shakespeare's time, though people behaved otherwise in their daily lives, they believed in God's final reckoning in the afterlife. Most contemporary audiences have trouble accepting Isabella's lines, "Then Isabel, live chaste; and brother die. More than our brother is our chastity" (2.4.184–85), as Shakespeare seems to have meant them to be taken. They have even more trouble with her stiff, angry, hateful response to Claudio when he wavers, seeking a way out of the death sentence, which he had earlier accepted as just. Seen against a background of seventeenth-century religious belief, however, Isabella's response to her brother's wavering is consistent with her character and virtue. Contemplating her threatened submission to rape and to loss of virginity (the price of Claudio's freedom), she insists, "O, were it but my life, I'd throw it down for your deliverance as frankly as a pin" (3.1.103–5). In Isabella's mind, to collude with Angelo in order to save Claudio would be to damn her immortal soul to hell, or to risk the doubly abhorrent possibility of bearing a child in sin and bastardy. Later, in hearing of Angelo's insistence that Claudio must die tomorrow, she is alarmed not that he must die but that he must die before his soul can be prepared for death, that he might go to meet his Maker before he is spiritually ready to do so. (Shakespeare heightens this point by contrast with the comic scenes of a Barnardine too drunk and stubborn to undergo final confession—and thus the jailors are helpless against his resistance.) No sooner does the Duke offer Isabella a plan to save Claudio that might *not* involve eternal damnation than she is ready and eager to pursue it to the utmost.

Other religious facets of the play lead to further problems. The Duke's adoption of a disguise as a Franciscan friar of Vienna was a way of distancing the time and place to get around political/religious censorship in Protestant England. The fact that Duke Vincentio fraudulently performs such sacred Catholic rites as confession and extreme unction (the preparation of the soul for dying) is highly problematic, even if, as he later asserts, it leads to processes of spiritual growth and purification. Later on in the play, the Duke's disguise also leads to the play's darkest moments, when he seems most manipulative. He cruelly and egotistically maintains his disguise as a friar when he could easily come forward as the Duke to stop the imminent execution of Claudio. Worse still, he tells Isabella that her brother has been executed, lying merely to reserve for himself the pleasure of making her "heavenly comforts" (4.3.97). There is more than a grain of truth in Lucio's apparent slander in referring to the Duke as "the duke of dark corners" (4.3.143–44). If directors and performers want to exonerate the Duke, they have to work hard to do so.

Though religious and political issues in the play present challenges to contemporary understanding, from another vantage point, such issues are especially relevant to our times: We have no shortage of sexual scandals in politics and public life, nor does our own culture lack a persistent double standard in matters of sexual conduct. These troubled springs of conflict in *Measure for Measure* have given the play a new, highly charged vitality in the twentieth and twenty-first centuries, when its potent clashes of will have been recreated in some electrifying contemporary performances.

Social Issues
in Literature

CHAPTER 3

Sexuality in the Twenty-First Century

Social Media and Choices in Relationships

Jill Filipovic

Jill Filipovic is a consultant, writer, speaker, and attorney who writes frequently about gender issues and the law. She also specializes in the business uses of social media.

In the following viewpoint, Filipovic critiques popular recent essays that lament the demise of traditional courtship and dating practices. Filipovic contends that while current courting and dating behaviors have their pitfalls, they also provide far more freedom, opportunity, and equality between the sexes. Women who are dating today are beneficiaries of gains in equality due to the feminist movement, and they currently benefit from the added freedom and opportunities provided by the explosion of social media.

It's practically a law: every few months, a major media outlet has to publish an anxious piece about "Women Today".

Women today are abandoning marriage; they're dying to get married. Women today can't balance work and family; they aren't having enough babies. Women today are doing better than men; women today can't have it all. The underlying theme is always the same: women today are miserable.

The latest play on this theme comes from the style section of the *New York Times* (the worst offender in the genre, except perhaps the *Atlantic* and the *Daily Mail*). The *Times* article asks if we are currently seeing "The End of Courtship?" (the implied answer, of course, is a resounding "yes"). Unfortunately, the *Times* is several decades late in discovering the demise of courtship.

The days when a man selected a woman for his mate and, by offering material gifts and a promise of marriage, "wooed her" are long gone. They were gone when my parents dated, my grandparents even. And thank goodness: the woman didn't get a whole lot of say in the courtship system; she was supposed to just be happy that someone was buying her things, and could take her off her father's hands.

No, the *Times* article is talking about the demise of *dating*. Fortunately, they needn't worry so much.

Changing Gender Roles and Technology

Despite the *Times'* hand-wringing, dating is still alive and well. It's just done slightly differently than it was a generation ago—much as that generation did things differently than the one before it, and on and on. Single people today have both changing gender roles and technology to fully skeeve out the folks who think that "change" is synonymous with "bad".

And make no mistake, things have changed. We have cell phones, which facilitate last-minute get-togethers. Platforms like Twitter and Facebook let you connect with a wide variety of people, and you can know someone's political leanings, interests, and hobbies before you ever meet in person. Online dating opens up a marketplace of singles, so you no longer have to rely only on your immediate social network to find a person of interest.

As with anything else, there are benefits and demerits to these advances. If your goal is to be fancily courted and then married at 22, that's certainly harder today than it was 50 years ago. But if your goal is to live a varied life, to learn about yourself through a variety of relationships, romantic and not, and to develop reasonably fully as a human being before you settle down, then there has never been a better time to be alive (especially as a woman).

Change is always scary, and I am sure plenty of commentators throughout history whined that the warmth of fire wasn't as satisfying as body heat, the flushing toilet less authentic than the chamber pot, the buggy not nearly as charming as the covered wagon. But alas, things change; humanity moves forward and adjusts. Young college students "pinning" their girlfriends in the 1950s was not exactly a centuries-old tradition. A more authentic marriage proposal—being sold into matrimony by your father, and taking few rights with you—is one that I'm sure most women are happy to leave behind.

Increasing Choices and Options

So, why this yearning for a past that, if it ever even existed, was only around for a short time? I suspect it's because rules, in many ways, are easier than freedom. Clearly delineated roles, no matter how suffocating, are simpler to navigate than a wide-open plain of choices and options.

Choices and options mean responsibility and possibility. They mean taking the reins of your own life. They mean things might sometimes be harder, but that the rewards might also be greater—might, might not.

That's terrifying.

And so we cling to a soft-focus ideal of yesteryear, when life was simple and we paired off easily, blushing on first dates before floating into domestic bliss.

Of course, that's not at all how it actually worked. The feminist gains of the 1960s and 70s were a reaction to those "blissful" 1950s. Women wanted their own bank accounts, the right to marry whom they pleased, a college education, a fulfilling career, control over when they had children, and the chance to pursue what they found inspiring. Lo and behold, women today are doing better than ever—especially the ones who graduate from college and marry later in life.

Feminist victories mean that women can enter into partnerships more equally. More egalitarian relationships tend to be more stable; partners in them have more sex; and the male partners tend to spend more time with their children. These pairings don't look like courtship, but they're good.

The Power of Social Media

Today's communication platforms also offer a wider variety of connections. Just looking at my immediate social circle, social media and gender equality have played a defining role: We've met long-term partners at professional conferences, through Twitter connections ("Hey, we've been tweeting at each other and I'm in town, wanna grab a drink?"), Facebook friends-of-friends, and online dating.

All of those media have their flaws, and in some instances, of course, filtering intimacy through the glow of a computer screen kills it—just as getting to know someone's myriad flaws up close and personal can kill an infatuation. But overall, a wider network seems better than a narrower one. More options may delay the process of picking one, but it seems to improve the chances of picking the right one, instead of simply settling for what's in front of you.

Before it sounds like I'm Pollyanna-ish about dating, let me be clear: I am 29, single, with a law degree and a writing career that takes up many of my waking hours (and formerly, a corporate legal career that took up many more of my waking hours, and quite a few of my sleeping ones). I am exactly the kind of woman who would wear a very severe bun in the first half of a romantic comedy. If you believe style section profiles, I should be mystified by dating rituals, cynical about my marriage prospects, and dedicated to spending the wee hours of any given Tuesday night downing Chardonnay and creating elaborate Pinterest wedding boards.

And yet, I think dating today is mostly great. Every single woman I know, including myself, goes on dates regularly. We have active and wonderful social circles. We complain about how hard it is to find love—and yet, that difficulty is exactly what makes love so special and desirable. We're open to romance, but we aren't crying over episodes of *Say Yes to the Dress*. Sometimes, a retro vision of dating makes it seem like an old-school model would be better, but I'm not sure any of us would actually make that trade.

With all of the social changes that have permeated the last century, there seems to be one constant: Dating is hard. Love stinks, except when it doesn't.

And for the record, it's a Wednesday and I'm downing Bordeaux.

The "Choice" Myth About Sexual Orientation

Ryan C. Ebersole

A mental health professional and counselor by training, Ryan C. Ebersole has written extensively on issues of sexuality and gender. Many of his articles can be found on the activist website Peoplesworld.org.

According to Ryan C. Ebersole, too many people accept the widespread argument that non-heterosexual orientation is no more than a "choice" that people make. Ebersole contends that this myth is perpetuated by conservative thinkers who use it as ammunition against equal rights for gays and lesbians, including the right to marry. This myth is also used to defend the controversial practice of trying to change a person's sexual orientation. In refutation of this myth, Ebersole points to the positions of the American Psychological Association and the American Psychiatric Association. Both organizations assess gay and lesbian behavior as "normal variations" within human sexuality, and they condemn attempts to change sexual orientation as "unscientific."

Since the advent of the gay rights movement, gay and lesbian people have been bombarded by a myth: that their non-heterosexual sexual orientation is nothing more than a "choice" that they made. This myth promotes the notion that sexual minority people are either disordered or sexual deviants. It is propped up by rhetoric from arch-conservative politicians and religious leaders who use it to oppose equal rights for gays and lesbians. However, it flies in the face of scientific truth (and logic).

Ryan C. Ebersole, "The 'Choice' Myth About Sexual Orientation," Peoplesworld.org, February 16, 2012. Reproduced by permission.

The myth that sexual orientation is a choice has been promulgated by right-wing Republicans and social Christian groups for years. This includes GOP candidates like Rick Santorum and Newt Gingrich. Santorum has referred to homosexuality as a "behavioral thing" that goes against "biblical truth." Gingrich also views sexual orientation as a choice, saying that gays and lesbians should choose to be "celibate" if they can't be heterosexual. In their defense of the Defense of Marriage Act, House Republicans allege that homosexuality is not "an immutable characteristic; it is behavioral."

The right-wing Christian group Focus on the Family claims that gays and lesbians can change their sexual orientation, claiming that biblical teaching holds homosexuality to be a violation of "God's intentional design for gender and sexuality." The Church of [Jesus Christ of] Latter-day Saints contends that while homosexuality or bisexuality may not be a conscious choice, it may be "treatable." The U.S. Conference of Catholic Bishops states that "homosexual inclinations" are "disordered."

The Myth of Changing Orientation

The choice myth also fuels a pseudo-scientific practice known as "reparative therapy," which seeks to change a person's sexual orientation via methods such as prayer, medical treatments and counseling. Exodus International, a "reparative therapy" Christian ministry, promotes these efforts around the United States and the world. This group promotes the notion of "ex-gays," gays and lesbians who they claim changed their sexual orientation.

The American Psychological Association (APA) has thoroughly condemned these efforts as without any scientific support. The APA states that such practices are at the very least ineffective and futile, and can often cause harmful psychological distress for the victim.

Former leaders of the "ex-gay" movement have admitted that "reparative therapy" does not work. Some have apologized for their hateful and dishonest rhetoric and actions. They also acknowledged that none of their "clients" ever actually changed their sexual orientation. Alan Chambers, one of the leaders of Exodus, admitted that Exodus International was a fraudulent institution.

A Normal Variation

What do actual psychological and medical organizations say about homosexuality? According to the American Psychological Association, homosexuality is a normal variation of human sexuality that does not indicate any disorder. The association goes on to say that sexual orientation is a romantic, emotional, and physical attraction to members of the same, opposite, or both sexes. The American Psychiatric Association opposes any "reparative therapy" because it has no record of efficacy, and is based on the incorrect premise that homosexuality is a disorder.

What does scientific research say about sexual orientation? Brain image scans have yielded distinct, observable differences between the brains of heterosexuals and the brains of their gay and lesbian peers. Positron emission tomography scans have indicated that the symmetry between brain lobes of gay men resembles those of heterosexual women. Researchers have also found that the amygdala (area of brain responsible for emotional learning) of gay men and straight women are similar, while the amygdala of straight men and lesbians are similar. According to Dr. Qazi Rahman, a professor of cognitive biology at Queen Mary University of London, these differences can only be formed during the fetal period, which indicates "if you are gay - you are born gay."

Inalterable Physical Differences

Another interesting distinction that has been observed is in finger digit ratio. The ratio between the index and ring finger has been linked to differences between homosexuals and heterosexuals. Lesbians and gay men tend to have observable differences in this ratio from their heterosexual counterparts. Digit length and ratio is determined in the womb by prenatal hormones. This evidence points to differences in prenatal hormone environments between gays, bisexuals and lesbians, and their heterosexual peers. Basically, there is nothing that can be done after a child is born that can alter these outcomes.

In fact, scientists have noted several inalterable physical differences between gays and lesbians and straights that cannot be explained by calling homosexuality a "choice." These include direction of one's hair whorl, pheromone preference, hypothalamic volume, and even penis size.

There is also something to be said for using logic when it comes to answering the question, "Do gays and lesbians choose their sexual orientation?" What would motivate such a choice? Is it exciting to be able to be legally fired for one's sexual orientation in 29 states? Is it cool to risk alienation and rejection from one's family and friends? How about the condemnation of many major religions? How about being bullied in school? When one applies logic and critical thinking, the answer to that question is a very easy and obvious "No."

So why, in the face of overwhelming evidence (and logic), do conservatives continue to spread the falsehood that sexual orientation is a choice? That is easy; it is for the same reason many of them compare homosexuality and bisexuality to negative behaviors like bestiality, incest and alcoholism—it helps them justify their opposition to basic civil rights and dignity for sexual minorities. It is much harder to blatantly discriminate if the characteristic in question is immutable, such as race or gender.

The Decline of Romantic Comedies in American Film

Christopher Orr

Christopher Orr is a senior editor and principal film critic at the Atlantic. He has written about movies and has worked as an editor for numerous other publications.

Orr argues in the following viewpoint that American romantic comedies are not nearly as good as they used to be. The best films in the genre date back to the 1930s; however, Orr contends there have been great "rom-coms" even in the 1990s. One of the main problems now is that the obstacle to wedded bliss has changed drastically. In older films, the obstacles were reliable problems such as parental disapproval, engagement to someone else, or difference in social class. Now, however, with the wider acceptance of premarital sex and more open social values, these obstacles have been replaced by wild, improbable ones, such as one potential mate is a prostitute, or is in a coma, or is a zombie. Orr concludes that the romantic comedy genre is inescapably stale.

The romantic comedy has fallen on tough times. After a decade of essentially printing money, the genre abruptly ran out of box-office steam in 2012. As the producer Lynda Obst, a rom-com doyenne (*Sleepless in Seattle, How to Lose a Guy in 10 Days*), told *New York* magazine's *Vulture* blog in December [2012], "It is the hardest time of my 30 years in the business." In a departure from Februaries gone by, the weeks leading up to Valentine's Day this year were devoid of a single helping of romantic froth featuring Drew Barrymore or Kate Hudson or any of the multitude of Jennifers. No *50 First*

Dates. No *Fool's Gold*. No *He's Just Not That Into You*. So what happened? A range of explanations have been offered, from studios ever more obsessed with blockbuster franchises to a generation of moviegoers less starry-eyed than their predecessors.

But this line of inquiry misses the point. The proper question isn't *Why have romantic comedies suddenly stopped being profitable?* but rather *Why have they been so lackluster for decades?* The fact that the 2009 Katherine Heigl vehicle *The Ugly Truth* made a great deal of money in no way alters the fact that it was atrocious. I am not by nature a cinematic declinist, and it's true that classics of the genre have been sprinkled across the years, from the bittersweet doubt of *Annie Hall*, to the ascending optimism of *When Harry Met Sally* and *Pretty Woman*, to the raunchy resuscitations of Judd Apatow. But when one thinks back on the works reliably churned out by the likes of [Spencer] Tracy and [Katharine] Hepburn and [Cary] Grant and the other Hepburn (apologies, Audrey— you, too, were one of a kind!), it's rather hard not to get dispirited.

A Question of Charisma

A few years ago, A.O. Scott of the *New York Times* suggested that for explanation we need look no further than the names just mentioned and others like them: the downslope from Katharine Hepburn to Katherine Heigl is simply too steep, and "the few remaining stars who show the kind of audacity and charisma that great romantic comedy requires tend to be busy with other things."

This is certainly true, but it in turn begs the question of why today's genuine stars (with all due respect to Kate Hudson and Matthew McConaughey) no longer bother to find the time for romantic comedy. Will Smith, for instance, displayed tremendous chops in *Hitch*—but apart from that toe-dip, he's stayed clear of the water. And this generation's most obvious fit, George Clooney, has modeled his career on that of Cary Grant in almost every way save his profound reticence to explore the genre that made the latter an icon.

No, there's more at work here than the vagaries of stars or studios. It's not just them; it's us.

The Obstacle to Bliss

Among the most fundamental obligations of romantic comedy is that there must be an obstacle to nuptial bliss for the budding couple to overcome. And, put simply, such obstacles are getting harder and harder to come by. They used to lie thick on the ground: parental disapproval, difference in social class, a promise made to another. But society has spent decades busily uprooting any impediment to the marriage of true minds. Love is increasingly presumed—perhaps in Hollywood most of all—to transcend class, profession, faith, age, race, gender, and (on occasion) marital status.

When Sydney Pollack, for example, made the disastrous decision to update the Billy Wilder classic *Sabrina* in 1995, one of the remake's (many) flaws was its failure to modernize the obsolete dilemma of the rags-and-riches romance. As Samuel Taylor, who wrote the original Broadway play and collaborated on Wilder's script, told the *New Yorker* at the time, "If they really wanted to make it interesting, they'd find a really good black actress to play [Sabrina]." Eighteen years later, of course, that wouldn't be enough. She'd have to be a mummy.

Perhaps the most obvious social constraint that's fallen by the wayside is also the most significant: the taboo against premarital sex. There was a time when carnal knowledge was the (implied) end point of the romantic comedy; today, it's just as likely to be the opening premise. In 2005's *A Lot Like Love*—a dull, joyless rip-off of *When Harry Met Sally*—Amanda Peet and Ashton Kutcher meet cute by having sex in an airplane

Romantic comedies, such as 50 First Dates, *starring Drew Barrymore and Adam Sandler (shown above), are declining in the American film industry due to a wider acceptance of premarital sex and more open social values regarding sexuality.* © Moviestore collection Ltd/Alamy.

lavatory before they've spoken a single word to each other. Where's a film to go when the "happy ending" takes place at the beginning?

More Bizarre Complications

Serious obstacles to romantic fulfillment can still be found—illness, war, injury, imprisonment—but they have a tendency to be just that: serious. There aren't likely to be many laughs, after all, in the story of a love that might be torn asunder by an IED [improvised explosive device]. It is perhaps no coincidence that romantic melodramas (such as last year's *The Vow* and the recent epidemic of Nicholas Sparks adaptations) are doing quite well at the multiplex even as their comic siblings falter.

So new complications must be invented, test-driven, and then, as often as not, themselves retired. (The idea that geography posed a substantial challenge to true love seemed a stretch all the way back in 1993, for *Sleepless in Seattle*. In the Internet age, it doesn't pass the laugh test.) The premises grow more and more esoteric: She's a hooker. He's a stalker. She's in a coma. He's telepathic. She's a mermaid. He's a zombie. She's pregnant. He's the president.

And if worst comes to worst—as it does, all too often—there's the ever-accommodating fallback that one partner is uptight and the other is a free spirit (if a woman) or a slob (if a man), requiring the two to work in tandem to respectively unwind and domesticate.

Exceptions to the Trend

Happily, the cinematic landscape is still dotted with exceptions, experiments in romantic chemistry that in many cases benefit from steering wide of the usual tropes. There's a case to be made that the two best romantic comedies of 2012 succeeded in large part because they weren't really framed as romantic comedies at all. David O. Russell's *Silver Linings Playbook* may have had a rom-com structure, but it was darker and more idiosyncratic, with a premise at once novel and true to life: Two lovers thwarted by mental illness. Better still was Wes Anderson's *Moonrise Kingdom*, which offered as its obstacle an ironic update of the old parental-disapproval plot: Young Sam and Suzy can't run off together and get married because *they're 12 years old*. (It's an obstacle that, incidentally, is not presented as insurmountable.)

One could argue that the easy profitability of the past decade was the worst thing to happen to the romantic comedy—an invitation to stale formulas and ridiculous conceits alike—and a few lean years might do the genre good. It was, after all, 75 years ago this Valentine's Day that Howard Hawks's comic masterpiece *Bringing Up Baby* opened in theaters—and bombed.

Modern Myths About Sex Differences

Agustin Fuentes

Trained in zoology and anthropology, Agustin Fuentes is a pro-
fessor of anthropology at the University of Notre Dame.

Most people operate with a range of false assumptions about
what it means to be male or female, according to anthropologist
Agustin Fuentes in the following viewpoint. Sex differences be-
tween men and women are biologically measurable, but gender,
which includes the roles and perceptions society places on the
sexes, operates on more of a masculinity-femininity continuum.
Even such physical features as genitals and brains have far more
biological similarities than differences. In fact, in aggression,
parenting instincts, and sexual desire, women and men are more
similar than people think.

Everyone knows that men and women are really different.
We think differently and act differently because we are
wired differently. I mean look at our brains and genitals: They
are just plain different. Right?

Wrong.

What if many of the things we assume about the biology
of difference are not so different at all? What if it is not our
"wiring" but the ways in which our bodies and minds develop
and play out in society that make us seem so unalike? Could
it be that men and women are more similar than we think?

Yes, women give birth and lactate and men do not. And
yes, men are, on average, slightly larger than women and usually have greater upper-body strength. There are these basic
biological differences between the sexes and they are impor-

tant ... but why always focus on the differences and not the biological, and behavioral, similarities? Ahh, that would be because of gender.

Gender is a powerful reality; it is the perception and expectation of differences between males and females and it shapes both our bodies and our society. Gender differences are real and important, but they are not hardwired or even static. There is no biological or evolutionary mandate that only women really care for babies and show emotions, or that males are the best at economics and politics and prefer beers and skirt-chasing to domestic bliss. These are patterns of gender roles and expectations that shape the ways we look at our biology and behavior. They influence the way we expect the world to be. It is the strength of the societal myths about sex that fool us into thinking that men and women are so different by nature.

So let's bust some of those myths.

1) Gender and Sex Are the Same Thing

Sex and gender are interconnected, but not the same thing. Sex is a biological state that is measured via what chromosomes you have (XX or XY, usually) and aspects of your body and physiology. Gender includes the roles, expectations and perceptions that a given society has for the sexes. Most societies have two genders on a masculinity-femininity continuum. Some have more. We are born with a biological sex, but acquire gender. There is a ton of individual diversity within societies and sexes in regard to how sex and gender play out in behavior and personality. There is an extensive body of data demonstrating this, but people interested only in specific differences between men and women choose to ignore it.

2) Male and Female Genitals Are Totally Different

Most people think that male and female genitals are about as different as can be: penis=male and vagina=female. But even this basic dichotomy is not quite correct: The genitals emerge from the same mass of embryonic tissue. For the first six weeks of life the tissue masses develop identically. At about 6-7 weeks, depending on whether the fetus has XX or XY chromosomes (usually), the tissues start to differentiate. One part of the tissues begins to form the clitoris or penis and another forms the labia or scrotum. Another area begins to form into either the testes or the ovaries. This means that physiologically, male and female genitals are made of the same stuff and work in similar ways.

3) Male and Female Brains Are Different

If there were really deep-seated differences between male and female human behavior and biology they should show up in the brain. The genitals start in the same place and end up looking different, the brain does not. Our brains are pretty much the same. Male brains are a bit bigger than females' (like their bodies) and females' brains stop growing earlier than males (as with their bodies). However, whatever one may believe about other organs, in the case of healthy brains, size really does NOT matter one iota. There also might be a few differences in a small part of the brain called the straight gyrus (need more testing in this one). Other than these minor aspects there are no consistent and replicated reliable differences in male and female brains; it is a human brain . . . but how we use it is another matter.

4) Hormones Make the Difference

Everyone thinks that males and females have different hormones . . . testosterone for men and estrogen for women. Nope, all the actual hormones in males and females are the same: There are no male-only or female-only hormones. Both men and women can get a flood of testosterone when they get into a fight or take part in an exhilarating sports match. Both men and women can get a flood of oxytocin and prolactin when they pick up a newborn baby. There can be differences in the levels, patterns, and impacts of some of these hormones in male and female bodies, but individual variation is often more important than the variation between the sexes.

5) Men Are More Aggressive than Women

It all depends what you mean by aggression. Men and women are not different in expressing anger and general aggression, but men are more likely to use physical aggression overall. The sexes are more or less the same when aggressing towards one another, but men are larger and, usually, stronger. Men are not naturally "more aggressive" than women, but can use physical aggression more effectively than women can (barring guns and other weapons). This pattern says more about gender, societies, and male physical size than it does about hardwired human nature.

6) Women Are Natural Parents and Men Are Not

Women give birth and men do not. Women lactate and men do not. However, both men and women have the same potential hormonal responses to infants (with a lot of variation between individuals). Human infants are amazingly helpless and needy and we know that throughout our species' history it has taken a lot of people to raise kids. Human bodies and minds are capable of parenting regardless of sex, and our entire history of success as a species is because both males and females (of all ages) have helped raise the next generation. Women give birth and nurse, but we can all care for children; neither sex automatically becomes a better parent than the other.

7) Men Want Sex More than Women

This is what most people assume . . . however, when researchers look at what people actually do, the data show that men and women have more or less the same amount of sex in the same kinds of ways across the life span (remember it does take two to tango). But there are some important differences in sexual interest. For example, married women report lower interest in sex with their husbands the longer they've been with them and younger men report higher frequencies of masturbation and interest in visual pornography. But are these really biological sex differences or something else? We still have a lot to learn about sexuality . . . and as with many other areas it looks like variation is highest between individuals, not between sexes.

8) Women Want Relationships More than Men

Not biologically speaking. . . . Both male and female bodies respond in the same ways to pair-bonding and there is no biological difference in patterns of attachment or desire. However, survey data suggest that men want many more partners over their lifetime than women. Nonetheless, if you look not at the average of male and female responses, but rather the median (the actual middle of the range of answers), both men and women are extremely close. This is because more men report extremely high numbers than do women and thus their average is higher. Is this biology or maybe a bit of gender roles rearing their head? In reality both men and women want to be with others in a wide range of sexual and emotional relationships . . . again individual variation is more than between the sexes.

For Further Discussion

1. On the basis of the evidence we have about Shakespeare—his poems, his plays, and the known facts of his life—do you think it is reasonable to draw conclusions about Shakespeare's own sexual orientation? Why or why not?

2. David Bevington contends that Shakespeare's romantic heroines are more savvy about love and sexuality than the young men of these plays. Do you think that, in this, Shakespeare is expressing some sort of universal truth, or is this idea a false generalization? Explain.

3. In the viewpoints of Penny Gay and Alexander Leggatt, the characters in *As You Like It* and *A Midsummer Night's Dream* fumble badly with the courtship process and make many mistakes. Do you think that the viewpoint by Jill Filipovic reveals a similar kind of courtship confusion today? Explain your reasoning.

4. According to Maurice Charney and Michael Mangan, *The Taming of the Shrew* and *Much Ado About Nothing* depict sexual tension and verbal combat as contributing to a healthy match between mates. In contrast, modern matchmaking services such as Match.com seek to pair people by their harmony and similarities. Which approach do you find healthier and why?

For Further Reading

William Shakespeare, *As You Like It*. Ed. Juliet Dusinberre. London: Arden Shakespeare, 2006.

William Shakespeare, *Hamlet*, in *The Complete Works of Shakespeare*, (7th ed.) Ed. David Bevington. Boston, MA: Pearson, 2013.

William Shakespeare, *King Henry IV, Part 1*. Ed. David Scott Kastan. London: Arden Shakespeare, 2002.

William Shakespeare, *King Lear*. Ed R.A. Foakes. London: Arden Shakespeare, 1997.

William Shakespeare, *Measure for Measure: Texts and Contexts*. Eds. Ivo Kamps and Karen Raber. Play edited by David Bevington. Boston, MA: Bedford/St. Martin's, 2004.

William Shakespeare, *Much Ado About Nothing*. Ed. Claire McEachern. London: Arden Shakespeare, 2006.

William Shakespeare, *Romeo and Juliet*. Ed. René Weis. London: Arden Shakespeare, 2012.

William Shakespeare, *Shakespeare's Sonnets*. Ed. Katherine Duncan-Jones. London: Arden Shakespeare, 2010.

William Shakespeare, *Twelfth Night*. Ed. Keir Elam. London: Arden Shakespeare, 2009.

William Shakespeare, *The Winter's Tale*. Ed. John Pitcher. London: Arden Shakespeare, 2010.

Bibliography

Books

Marina Adshade — *Dollars and Sex: How Economics Influences Sex and Love.* San Francisco, CA: Chronicle Books, 2013.

Susan Dwyer Amussen — "The Family and the Household," in *A Companion to Shakespeare*, ed. David Scott Kastan. Oxford, UK: Blackwell Publishers, 1999.

Jonathan Bate — *Soul of the Age: A Biography of the Mind of William Shakespeare.* New York: Random House, 2009.

David Bevington — "Love's Labour's Lost and Won," in *Shakespeare's Comedies of Love*, eds. Richard Paul Knowles and Karen Bamford. Toronto: University of Toronto Press, 2008.

David Bevington — *Shakespeare: The Seven Ages of Human Experience.* Malden, MA: Blackwell, 2005.

Maurice Charney — *Shakespeare on Love and Lust.* New York: Columbia University Press, 2000.

David Daniell — "The Good Marriage of Katherine and Petruchio," in *The Taming of the Shrew: Critical Essays*, ed. Dana E. Aspinall. New York: Routledge, 2002.

Marjorie Garber   *Shakespeare After All*. New York: Pantheon Books, 2004.

Shirley Nelson Garner   "Male Bonding and the Myth of Women's Deceptions in Shakespeare's Plays," in *Shakespeare's Personality*, eds. Norman N. Holland, Sidney Homan, and Bernard J. Paris. Berkeley: University of California Press, 1989.

Alan Haynes   *Sex in Elizabethan England*. Stroud, UK: Sutton, 2006.

Anthony Holden   *William Shakespeare: The Man Behind the Genius: A Biography*. Boston, MA: Little, Brown, 2000.

Lisa Hopkins   "Marriage as Comic Closure," in *The Shakespearean Marriage: Merry Wives and Heavy Husbands*. New York: St. Martin's Press, 1998.

Peter Hyland   *An Introduction to Shakespeare: The Dramatist in His Context*. New York: St. Martin's Press, 1996.

Alexander Leggatt, ed.   *The Cambridge Companion to Shakespearean Comedy*. New York: Cambridge University Press, 2002.

Michael Mangan   *A Preface to Shakespeare's Comedies: 1594–1603*. New York: Longman, 1996.

Marianne Novy   *Love's Argument: Gender Relations in Shakespeare*. Chapel Hill: University of North Carolina Press, 1984.

Phyllis Rackin

Shakespeare and Women. New York: Oxford University Press, 2005.

W. Reginald Rampone Jr.

Sexuality in the Age of Shakespeare. Santa Barbara: CA: Greenwood, 2011.

Lawrence R. Samuel

Sexidemic: A Cultural History of Sex in America. Lanham, MD: Rowman & Littlefield, 2013.

Michael Schoenfeldt

"Friendship and Love, Darkness and Lust: Desire in the Sonnets," in *The Cambridge Introduction to Shakespeare's Poetry*. Cambridge: Cambridge University Press, 2010.

Erich Segal

"*Twelfth Night*: Dark Clouds over Illyria," in *The Death of Comedy*. Cambridge, MA: Harvard University Press, 2001.

Dan Slater

Love in the Time of Algorithms: What Technology Does to Meeting and Mating. New York: Current, 2013.

Valerie Traub

"Gender and Sexuality in Shakespeare," in *The Cambridge Companion to Shakespeare*, eds. Margreta de Grazia and Stanley Wells. Cambridge, UK: Cambridge University Press, 2001.

Stanley Wells

Looking for Sex in Shakespeare. New York: Cambridge University Press, 2004.

Stanley Wells

Shakespeare, Sex, and Love. New York: Oxford University Press, 2010.

Periodicals and Internet Sources

Guttmacher Institute   "Facts on American Teens' Sexual and Reproductive Health," June 2013. www.guttmacher.org/pubs/FB-ATSRH.html.

Stephen Orgel   "Nobody's Perfect; or Why Did the English Stage Take Boys for Women?," *South Atlantic Quarterly*, vol. 88, 1989, pp. 7–29.

John Tierney   "A Match Made in the Code," *New York Times*, February 11, 2013.

Index

CPSIA information can be obtained
at www.ICGtesting.com
Printed in the USA
FFOW05n0659140814

9 780737 769838